ESTER PA...

MACRAME

FOR BEGINNERS

YOUR STEP-BY-STEP GUIDE TO CREATE UNIQUE & EASY DIY PROJECTS FOR HOME&GARDEN. THE ANCIENT ART TO LEARN THE BASIC KNOTS & TECHNIQUES TO MAKING STUNNING JOBS WITH MODERN TRICKS

TABLE OF CONTENTS

INTRODUCTION

My name is Ester and I live in Ohio with my family. I am an American craftswoman and I write books because I love my work and I want to teach it to others. Among the various arts I make, I learned about and made my first projects in Macramé a few years ago.

Like the venerable art of tying knots in a range of patterns, Macramé essentially produces beautiful adornments or accessories that we can wear around the house or in our daily activities. Macramé was a sensation in pop culture from the 1970s through the 20th century, and it is now coming back as we navigate in this present time.

Adopting a boho chic style means recreating the environment in which you live under the banner of nature, freedom and nonconformity.

From the hippy culture, it takes the light clothing made of macramé, natural fibers and light fabrics that leave the body free, but also the idea of deep love for nature and between people.

A self-respecting boho clothing includes the use of linen clothes, silk, and can not miss chiffon, macramé jewelry, brooches and bracelets preferably handmade.

The colors that best resemble the boho chic style are the most muted and natural.

Maybe, Macramé will become popular again because it is easy to learn. As you learn and master the knots and Macramé techniques, you can move on to more complex and incredible projects. Macramé is a boundless craft since it is an acceptable form of workout for the fingers and wrist. Your joints will persist to be robust when subjected to the movements of Macramé knots. Macramé is also great for taking off pressure and relaxing at the end of the day. You will sense tranquility and satisfaction after several knots, which translates into a gratifying feeling when you see your work's results.

History of Macramé

Travelers make fringes for wheel covers and bells, watches, and screens. Much of the history of Macramé is colored like fibers and beds used. Macramé essentially creates more space in a project. The pieces that complete the art works can be considered for their complexity and the technologies used, and the design created. Parts of the Macramé projects are created by connecting cords. Ordered knots generate a pattern, and this single pattern creates an overall look, mainly if the object uses a lot of glossy, colored beads. However, if you want to know where and when Macramé started, you will appreciate a short trip to this fine art's basics. The old history of Macramé is a bit overdone. There is little evidence that Macramé was introduced in France and Italy during the 14th and 15th centuries. France produced a large amount of Macramé, and historical data shows that it was notable for the set image. Macramé was very popular among British and North American sailors in the 19th century who spent long hours on ships, connecting rectangular ships and moving ships. They sold those artworks in India and China. Macramé is believed to have been introduced to England in the late 17th century by Queen Mary, who built a business in Holland. In 1780, Queen Charlotte, wife of George III, was busy constructing Macramé groups for court decorations. Macramé continued to make itself known worldwide, and many cultures have had the same weirdness they used in their native art.

In the early 20th century, Macramé focused on many functional items, such as bags, belts, leashes, lanyards, light and shade trains, and bells. Simultaneously, local artists in Portugal, Ecuador, and Mexico continue to make needles and handbags as native crafts. In North America, Macramé became a popular craft among hippie generations and children of the 1970s through the 1960s and 1970s. Macramé sales decreased in the 1980s, and soon, the art was forgotten. But not today, as Macramé and boho style are making a massive comeback among people of all ages.

CHAPTER 1

MACRAMÉ BENEFITS

Do you realize that hobbies can minimize tension by 34 percent? That is good! Even escaping from the humdrum routine and doing something enjoyable will greatly benefit your well-being. Improve your psychological health with a calming exercise: Macramé. There is no question that this year is going to be a major year for Macramé. To someone who wants to knit or crochet, this is the ideal hobby concept.

Essentially, it means making a variety of glamorous boho pieces utilizing knotting techniques—such as wall decor, jewelry, plant hangers, handbags, and more. To get going, just invest in a braided cotton string loop.

Whether you choose to take up a relaxing game, Macramé is a perfect way to unlock your ingenuity, stimulate your brain, and alleviate tension. Although it's relaxing and entertaining as a sport, Macramé often has a particular function—the final product presents you with anything you can confidently show for art or sale or send to your friends and family as a thoughtful, personalized gift.

Macramé will allow you to turn yourself into a profitable business, like I did by opening my own little store.

However, its healing properties will have you hooked since making everything with your hands is inspiring.

You may also use Macramé as a regular method of meditation. You will start to experience and appreciate the flow and repetition of knotting a pattern as you become more immersed and involved in this beautiful work.

What is more, Macramé does not need a ton of equipment—all you need is a wire, scissors, hands, and anything to hang on. Additionally, there are several resources and things that can support you and save time. The description that has been extended on each object is shown below, and you can understand why it is helpful to be applied.

It Serves as a Relaxing Therapy

Stress therapy has been popular in the world today. With the rise in so many activities and the busy schedules of many, there is a need to bring balance through actions that can calm the nerves and reduce tension. Depression and anxiety are other emotional problems that need serious attention. Macramé art is an effective way of managing such stressful situations. The processes involved in creating a piece of Macramé art take your attention away from the stress and emotional imbalances and focus them on the art of crafting. The joy of having to create something beautiful is a good way of taking off unnecessary stressors.

As you craft different forms of Macramé art, it helps you meditate. This meditation brings about peace and calmness in your entire body. This is why many people who are Macramé crafters are most time joyful. As you create different materials, it indirectly affects the neurons that are secreted in your brain. So, even when the emotions you are feeling at that point are depressing emotion, your brain can secret other hormones that trigger up happiness and joy within you. The more time you spend making Macramé, the more your mood and state of mind transform for the better.

It Boosts your Mental Capacity

For many people, Macramé means different things. For some, the skill of creating something that appeals to the eyes is both mental and intellectual. Intellectual in the sense that the individual has to come up with an excellent design that makes his works stand out. This process indirectly increases your brain power and cognitive reasoning. You can use it as a medium to awaken your critical reasoning power, especially when you feel you are gradually losing control over it as a result of pressures from the office or family. Today so many have been celebrated on account of the beautiful pieces of art they have created. Sometimes you might not have all the necessary material to finish your design. Your ability to improvise and make use of what you have can boost your thinking capacity. Many of the early crafters of Macramé, like the sailors, didn't always have all the desired components to build something nice. They only got the opportunity when they arrived in some cities and docked at some bays. This didn't also stop them from creating better designs because they made use of the available materials.

It Strengthens your Arms

Tying Macramé knots and patterns help strengthen your arms and muscles. For persons who have begun experiencing conditions that weaken their arms and muscles, Macramé knot tying can be used to bring back their strength. As you continue tying and knotting, you will find yourself gently receiving relief from your pain and muscle contractions. You will also discover your joints becoming free and loose.

It Enhances Creativity

Everyone is creative; all you need is to trust and believe in yourself to unlock that part of your brain. You are free to express yourself in what you make, and therefore this allows you to engage your creative side and make breathtaking Macramé pieces.

It Helps you Grow

The art of Macramé is great because just like any other art; it is a wonderful way to meet people and learn more about the world around you. It motivates you to get out of your comfort zone and try new exciting skills. It challenges your thinking and makes you better.

Once you are out of your comfort zone, growing with each day, you start to grow and become a better person. Learning Macramé allows you to live an active, healthy, and connected life, as you spend time learning what other people are doing, get inspired by their crafts, find ways of improving or customizing them, and more.

It Gives you Time to Learn a New Skill

People are always looking to learn new beneficial skills. By learning Macramé, you build a new skill that is not only fun but also very beneficial to you.

It is always challenging to try something new because you are not used to the change. Therefore, to make it more interesting and fun, you need to try something that challenges you while at the same time being enjoyable.

Macramé offers just that—the perfect combination of challenges and fun as you slowly become better knot by knot. Once you create something nice, you will feel quite happy and satisfied that you will love engaging in Macramé.

It Allows You to Make Amazing Works of Art

Macramé is a great form of art that allows you to create beautiful works of art. Many things you can make from Macramé, such as wall hangings, jewelry, clothes, or even sandals. Being able to create something just the way you want it is good because you will be satisfied and content with it.

It Is a Way to Make a Living Easily

If you've been looking for a way to make a living by doing your own business, then Macramé is the way to go. People are always looking for ways to decorate their offices and homes, and with the fact that you can create unique pieces that inspire and ooze elegance, you could quickly sell your crafts to people. People love beautiful things, irrespective of how the economy is performing! So, if you can perfect this skill, you could make it your little side hustle, which could easily pay some bills for you, and if you are serious about it and become a pro at Macramé, you could even turn it into a full-time business, as you make breathtaking works of art that people will not say no to.

CHAPTER 2

MATERIALS NEEDED

Natural Materials

Natural materials for Macramé are still very common choices. They have properties that are very different from conventional materials that you need to know if you want to use them. This contains a description of today's most common natural cord materials and yarns made from natural fibers, too.

Hemp Material

Hemp twine is the most common of all the natural products used for Macramé. The natural color here in the back is light brown. Dyed hemp comes in colors that are single or mixed. Hemp products are produced from the outer bark of the plant genus Cannabis Sativa, one of the fastest-growing plants.
There are three types of hemp: twine, rope, and yarn. We each have different properties, so I will separately explain them.
Hemp Rope usually has a diameter of 1 mm to 3 mm and is determined by size instead of weight. A size of 3mm is sometimes referred to as "Spring Cord" because it is often used in spring mattress construction.

Properties

Hemp fibers are mold and mildew-resistant, which makes them distinct from other natural materials.
Hemp YARN is solid so flexible, but not like knitting yarn. In the way this bends, it is similar to cotton. This creates perfect, solid knots keeping their form.
Hemp CORD begins as a yarn made of several twisted fibers. The strings are then twisted to form the cord together. So, it's twisted double, which makes it much more effective. It's not easy to find, and the natural brown color is usually.

Cotton

Cotton is the most versatile of all the natural materials used in Macramé. You can use it for big items like hammocks and fine jewelry suspensions. Cotton is the softest of all naturally occurring fabrics. Cotton cords may be solid and flexible. So much washing and drying tend to wear it out. Handbags and clothes from Macramé should be washed by hand and air-dried. This material creates strong ties that are uniform. There is minimal stretching, which is important to hold weight when making items. Cotton intensity improves when it is wet. Yet that's not how it should stay because it's going to get rotten. Sunlight affects cotton, which can make it look yellowish and cause it to degrade. Keep the material protected and check periodically for signs of rotting or cracking when using outdoor products.

Jute Twine

Jute twine is the least common of all the natural materials available for Macramé. Finding a good quality jute material is very hard and will be the same width in the roll. It will be cool, too, with a bit of shine. Jute is a plant with a high content of cellulose and wood fiber. It is woven into compressed and twisted coarse threads to form cords. Many jute fiber fabrics are used to make inexpensive burlap bags, carpets, chairs, canvas, etc. Often jute fibers are mixed with other materials for making clothes and household furniture. One thing people like is the blurred quality of it. Jute's going to have SMALL tendrils of good quality. Colored Jute is difficult to find, but online shops carrying packaging can have it.

Size

The natural materials are also sold by the number of fibers that make up the PLY cord. Jute, ply, and weight defines the sizes, making it very confusing. The scale of the producer also varies.

Properties

This course content, even in the heavy-weight format, is strong and surprisingly flexible. The weights of the medium make strong knots. The heavyweight will take more effort, but the knots will still be fairly tight. Jute's strength will decrease if it's muddy. This is also quickly biodegradable. That's why this isn't the perfect choice for outdoor projects. Finding good quality content is the most difficult thing with a jute cord.

Linen Cord

The linen cord is a special flax plant fiber. It's not as common as other natural materials. Because it is mainly used for jewelry, it is often carried by online stores. The cellulose fibers just below the bark of the flax (stem) plant are collected first, then spun into threads and yarns. We then make clothes, bedding, and household things.

Style

Flax linen cord is normally a material of twist style. These are highly flexible, producing tight knots. Usually, the natural color is gray, yellow-gold, or brown. It can also be used in some colors. A waxed cord of linen is an excellent beading and micro-Macramé option. Flax cord material, similar to lacing, may often have a flat profile. For this style, you can still tie knots, but you have to work a bit more for the cord so that they fold and bend easily.

Silk Cord

It is possible to produce natural products from animals. Moth larvae originating in northern China are produced from soil called Silkworm. Every cocoon is made of 1,000–2,000 feet long, continuous thread of raw silk filament. Silk has been used in clothing, art, and decorations in ancient China. Back then, as it is now, it was a luxury material. Creating 1 yard/meter of fabric requires around 3,000 coconuts. Instead of its increased cost after World War 2, synthetic materials were created to replace silk. Several countries still produce genuine silk, but it is still expensive.

Properties

Silk is the most powerful of all-natural materials. It has a shiny but not slippery, soft texture. Typically, it stays that way if the cord/thread is extended. When wet or exposed to sunlight for long periods, it is weakened. Silk is delicate, given its strength. So, when dealing with it, use the cross-pin method (or no pins at all). You may also roll and stitch the seed to form the cord.

Leather Cord

Leather is made of animals as well. This has somewhat different characteristics than other natural materials. Cattle are primarily raised for food, but all parts, including the hide, are used. Leather is made of hides and skins in different shapes. To avoid decomposition, leather is tanned. This is done using several ingredients, many of which are natural products such as tree bark and leaves. With brains or other fatty substances, buckskin is tanned. Chromium is the most common chemicals used for tanning. Leather is stabilized, thin, lubricated after tanning. This is known as crusting. It may be done in various ways, gently painted.
Not all leather is made of cattle: Fish leather is made of fish species' skin and scales. Deerskin leather is made of skins of deer. You can even find pig, elephant, alligator, lizard, squirrel, ostrich, kangaroo, leather, among other species.

Size

Leather cord comes in so many sizes, but it's really hard to make knots if it's longer than 2 mm. The best size for jewelry is between 1 mm and 1.5 mm.

Properties

Leather is incredibly strong but very fragile as well. Because the holes are permanent, you must not pass pins through the material. The cord of leather on the skin is very smooth and comfortable. It's not very good at breathing, so you should use your designs as little as you can. The natural color of bovine leather is brown, but in many colors, you can also get it. The shape of the knots is better in leather than any other cord material. Also, loosely bound knots will maintain their form. Similar to other natural materials, leather is not versatile. Tightening knots with material over 2 mm long is very difficult. That's the biggest reason why it doesn't make big Macramé items.

Natural Yarns

Natural materials include different types of yarn that can be used for projects in Macramé.

Size

Most yarns are priced by weight, so it's difficult to assess the material's actual width before you get it and measure it. Just a few brands will show the exact width, so quantity in the roll on the label. Keep in mind that the yarn is so compact that the knots are smaller than expected.
Normally, wool yarn can be stretched, and when released, this will spring back. The material repels moisture and is therefore flammable. Merino wool is extra soft, not as scratchy as other wool yarn types.
Alpaca yarn is cool and more refined than wool. It's not prickly either, and it doesn't have lanolin. It is also considered to be hypoallergenic. Some brands are brilliant.
Bamboo yarn is another special kind of natural fiber made from the bamboo plant's pulp. It's strong, very flexible, and can be as soft as silk. It's got a perfect natural shine. It makes very tight, tiny knots. Pins will damage bamboo yarn, so treat it as if you were going to use some fragile material and use the Cross-Pin Technique or no pins at all.
For any kind of yarn, using tape is not recommended.

Synthetic Materials

Synthetic means that the fibers are made by a chemical process.

CHAPTER 3

TOOLS AND EQUIPMENT

Macramé Boards

Macramé projects have to be fastened to a surface as you work, usually using a T pin or masking tape. It makes it easier to work with the cords, and it also helps to keep the ties secure and correctly positioned. In the nearest craft store or bead, or from online stores, specifically made Macramé frames are accessible, and they work for most designs. They are usually around 12 inches/18 inches (30 cm/46 cm) and are built of fiberboard. Many Macramé boards created have a graph on the surface and rulers along the edges. They can be replaced, but it's better to keep them in place using seals or shrink-wrapped because they can be handy directions when working on a project. Some other boards also include instructive diagrams of the basic knots in the Macramé.

Tape and Pins

Pins are being used to protect the Macramé board project, so it wouldn't shift about while you are working. These also come in handy when you integrate different knot patterns and other design features into your designs to keep other strings in position.

The most common alternative for Macramé is t-pins. They are good in scope, and their form makes it convenient to place and remove again and again. It is also possible to use ball-end pins used for embroidery, but they are not as durable as T-pins. Resist replacing push pins and thumbtacks, which are both too small.

Scissors

Most Macramé creations are composed of thin fibers that are easy to cut with a simple pair of art scissors like those you likely do own. You need to get a set of tiny cleaning scissors made for stitching to cut the extra length when a task is done. They will let you get close to whatever knot you want to miss.

Adhesives

Most Macramé projects are finished by securing the final knot(s) with adhesives. The type of adhesive that will be used would depend on the materials involved. Hemp, waxed linen, silk, cotton, and other fabrics are perfect for white glue. Leather and suede are ideally suited for rubber cement or touch cement. E-6000 and epoxy are very strong adhesives used to glue non-porous items together, such as labradorite beads or wire, which are used with the strap of the heart belt. Any of these adhesives require adequate airflow while in use and should be enforced strictly by all health warnings. The most favored type is the third! A powerful and durable, non-toxic, water-based super glue. Bear in mind the toxicity of the glue when choosing which glue is better to use for your project, mainly if it may come into contact with your skin.

Findings

These are all the small pieces, usually made of metal, used to create and complete jewelry items and other accessories. Some of the findings are used to conceal the things that are freshly made. Some of the results are used to protect the rough ends of strings, so it is essential to select the proper shape and size. Keep a broad range of findings in your workbox so you can build and complete various items.

The Finishing Ends

We use these findings to finish the edges of knotted strings. There are increasing numbers of designs being produced year after year, and the majority are available in a variety of shiny textures. For better outcomes, fit the cord or braid to suit the inner measurements of the finishing ends. Some finished limitations contain a clasp, but if not, you may add it yourself.

Cord Ends

This type is used to finish individual cords with lugs that you attach with clamps over the string; some are tubular and are therefore sealed with glue or by an internal crimping ring.

Spring Ends

It is one of the older finding types. It may be conical or cylindrical. Wrap the string or braid inside the wire coil, and use wire cutters to pinch just the end circle to seal it.

Cones End

Some cone-shaped or bell-shaped findings may either have a small hole at the top or end in a loop. Use jewelry glue to protect the braid in all designs for better results.

End Caps

End caps are rectangular, circular, or cylindrical styles of an end cone, with either a hole at the top edge or are ready-to-finish with a ring or circle. Use jewelry glue to protect the braid in all designs for better outcomes.

Trigger Clasp

This cheap spring-closure fastening is ideal for both necklaces and bracelets finishing. The lobster claw and a bolt ring are some of the available designs.

Multi-Strands Fasteners

Multi-strands fasteners come in a variety of types. The box kind is perfect for necklaces, and for Macramé and other cuff-style bracelets, the slider fastening is best. Select the number of rings on either side to suit your project.

Plastic Fasteners

These plastic clasps are explicitly made for knotting techniques such as crochet or Macramé since they have a bar end to tie the cords.

Beads

Without beads, most Macramé creations will not be complete. The accessible bead choices are stunning. The range of beads to deal with was small when the Macramé started. Since exchange has spread across the globe and technological advances, the beads that jewelry designers have to pick from nowadays are almost limitless.

CHAPTER 4

HOW TO FIND THE PERFECT ROPE

A Macramé cord comprises tangled or braided fibers/strands that bind or knot together to create a Macramé recognized as a textile craft.
Most of you who are only starting will also read or hear either Macramé yarn, strings, or rope referred to as Macramé cord. Usually, the Macramé cord has been used with such synonyms synonymously.

Macramé Cord Selection

It can be daring for new learners to realize what each term says, so let's dig further into the Macramé cord and the numerous forms of cables you must know about. That way, for future projects, you can select the right cord.
We had no concept; there were various cord styles when we first began Macramé. We thought it was just some plain-Jane string, and it's just required to create a Macramé. We didn't know about all types of fibers for the projects that can be included. Little did we realize, not all Macramé cords are produced similarly.
Let's have it broken down. The 3 different Macramé cord styles include:
• Braided
• Single Strand
• 3-ply / 3 Strand
Any of the Macramé projects would always fall under these types.

Braided Cord

Most beginners would start by buying a braided cord as it's the most inexpensive and simplest way to start Macramé. Generally, several art shops and major box retailers sell braided cords. Whenever they want to start immediately, several people rush to their nearest shop to get any chord they might find. After finishing a few Macramé projects, they would soon learn that a braided cord isn't the most appropriate thread for Macramé making. The reasoning is that the braided string is simply a rope of cotton, polypropylene, polyester, nylon, or other sturdy fibers.

It's cool to bind stuff together and offer it a firm grip, but it's hard to un-knot and fringe from it.

This is not a poor place for getting started using a braided cord with all that already said. It gets the work finished, and you will wind up with a project that is decently accomplished. You will find yourself switching either with 3-ply/the most widely used Macramé cord, the single-strand cord.

The usage of the Macramé rope and cord can also be heard. Usually, they are arguing about a similar topic. We distinguish between the 2 because the thread is braided/3-ply cord typically and the cord is the all-encompassing phrase for fibers, yarn, and string.

Single Strand Macramé Cord

If you plan to get into Macramé as a daily activity or full-time job, the single-strand cotton string is the best kind of Macramé cord by far to pick from. Usually, more costly is the single-strand cord, but if you don't like to splurge on the expensive thread right now, find some inexpensive cotton string on amazon and begin with those. It's easy on the hand, and it's going to be nice to learn. It would make unraveling knots, tying knots, cutting the cord, and cord fringing far simpler.

Macramé 3-Ply or 3-Stands Cord

The 3-ply is often pointed to as the cord of 3-stands. It consists of three smaller threads that shape a wide, twisted yarn. Macramé artists will also learn to utilize 3-ply/4-ply Macramé strings, which only implies the number of threads tied together to create a single cord strand.

That's what is known as multiply because you may get strands 4, 5, or 6-all twisted together to shape one strand until you begin moving through Macramé strings that are far more than three strands. There are four strands tied together to create a single rope strand.

Now, as you know, the three Macramé cord forms, let's explore four main points while choosing to use what Macramé cord for your Macramé and what you should search for.

Composition Macramé Cord
Natural/Synthetic Fiber

The composition of Macramé rope breaks into two units, synthetic or natural fibers.

Fibers generated naturally in the atmosphere are natural fibers. Plants, organisms, or natural features create them. Cotton, jute, linen, hemp, and wool are examples of natural fibers.

Every one of these fabrics can be broken down and reused naturally.

Synthetic fibers are the other choice. Synthetic fibers are composed of tiny molecules from synthetic polymers. The substances used to produce these fabrics originate from raw resources, such as petrochemicals or chemicals based on petroleum. Nylon, spandex, and polyester are also types of synthetic fibers.

Texture Macramé Cord

You can find that spool of cord has a different feel, texture, and finish to it if you've seen a lot of Macramé cords. It is a vital aspect of understanding the Macramé cords to feel the various forms of cord texture.

The more Macramé parts you create, the quicker you realize textures in all your Macramé designs play a huge role.

If you are trying to make the purchase online on a Macramé cord, try various brands to see what design suits you. You will notice that not every cotton cord made of Macramé is equal. The texture and feel of the threads can differ from manufacturer to manufacturer.

Macramé Cord Size
Diameter and Length

When doing your ideal Macramé project, understanding cord size is reasonably necessary. In the artistic presentation of Macramé designs, the scale of the cord plays a key function.

On Macramé cord sizes, we will not be moving into great depth.

Macramé cord is split down into three size groups for simplicity-small, medium, and large.

- Small Macramé Cord is usually the 1 to 2 mm diameter cord. You can also see these strings utilized in creating jewelry to the thread by beads and buttons and small-detailed art projects.

- Med Macramé Cord is where most of all Macramé designs are produced. Usually, it is from 3mm to 5mm. Quite commonly, 3mm or 4mm will often go. Certain measurements are also used for lanterns, wall hangings, plant hangers, rugs, curtains, etc.

- Large Macramé Cords are the pieces of your Macramé. This is going to be inside the range of something over 6 mm. These big sizes are typically used for covering broad space areas. The knots appear to be fewer, however still bigger.

For Macramé, What Cord Are You Using?

The response is the simplest: it varies.

We would consider using the Single Strand Cotton Cord of 3mm-4mm. If you have tried some projects utilizing cheaper cords, and now you are happy investing in a more excellent thread for better quality projects; then, you might be right with a single strand cord. If you are a new user and would like to start using the correct thread directly, you should do it as well.

We would consider using a single strand cord because it will increase our experience with Macramé. Tying knots and unraveling them is going to be less of a battle. Cutting cords and fringing will not have to sound like hard work, and the Macramé designs would be aesthetically appealing, most significantly.

Beginners in Macramé / Occasional Knotters

In their Macramé path, we realize not everybody is at the same point, so our advice does not extend to everybody. We would consider using some rope that we have laid around to practice if we are new to this art. If not, get some inexpensive cord from the nearest craft shop or grab some from Amazon if you are ready to start straight away. This Amazon cord is nicer than the thread that can be bought in the nearest craft shop—using this cord to learn tying ties, shapes, and series with Macramé. To get you started, that is the cost-effective cord of Macramé. To get a feel for creating the knots, begin to make smaller Macramé crafts like keyrings or Macramé feather designs.

Lovers And Enthusiasts of Macramé

We will suggest good quality 3mm or 4mm Single Strand Cotton Cord for those looking to improve their Macramé knotting skills and highlight their projects.

Alongside the uninterrupted fringing, knotting's smooth feel and simplicity allow it to use the best kind of Macramé cord. We will use this for 99 percent of our projects of Macramé.

The maximum Macramé cotton cord is accessible online from Bochiknot Macramé. If you are trying to begin on Macramé designs, there will be plenty of string to get you moving with one spindle of a 3mm single-strand cotton cord.

Two to three mid-sized Macramé projects should be done easily by one spool of Macramé cord. If you are searching for only a little extra, two spools will be enough to cover the current and future Macramé projects, so you don't run out of Macramé string.

CHAPTER 5

How to Deal with Large Tapestries

Macramé is one of the most popular forms of handwork in the world, one that has seen a resurgence in recent years. This will teach you what to do when your project becomes too large for you.

You are the Macramé maker. You are the designer of your Macramé project. No one else has to tell you what to do. That means that you are the one who decides when a project is finished, how big it will be, what color it will be, who or what it will represent, and more. Macramé is an art form in which you can put your stamp on things. Is one of the reasons I love it!

Here are pointers you can follow when you need to deal with large tapestries:

- Whenever you have to deal with a large piece of work, you must have everything that you need close at hand. Put all your tools, yarn, foam boards, etc., where they can be easily reached.

- Make sure your work surface is large enough to handle your project. You may have to place your project on a board so that you can keep it flat and wrinkle-free while working on it. Be sure the board has no sharp edges that could damage the yarn or interfere with your Macramé designs or patterns.

- Make sure you have a supply of adhesive tapes and spray glue on hand. You will be working with these materials to attach things, such as foam boards and yarns, to the tapestry.

- Create a plan of attack and measure exactly how big your project is before you even begin work on it. This is one of the most important steps when dealing with large tapestries. The best way to do this is to use a string or rope that will be long enough for you to hang the finished tapestry from one end and then measure out exactly how long the other end should be.

- A helpful hint is to use a piece of tape to mark the place where you will be making a significant change in a color or a design. You can then count the number of stitches from the place you started marking. That way, when you need to know how far away from your earlier stopping point you are, it will be easy for you to find out.

- Whenever possible, work with yarns that have been manufactured specifically for Macramé projects. Some yarns are made from materials that will easily stretch and break, which means your project will come apart before it is finished. Others are made from materials that do not easily stretch and will crack when stressed. Always use specialized yarns made for Macramé projects.

- When planning your project, make sure you take into consideration the weight of your work or tapestry. You should always use lightweight yarn when you are dealing with tapestries that weigh more than 100 pounds (45 kg). Unless you want to snap the yarn in half, don't work with heavier yarns on a big project.

- Always measure carefully before you start to work with a tapestry that is too large for you to handle or move around quickly. A tape measure is the best tool to use when measuring a big project.

- Try to keep one end of your tapestry out of the way while you are working with the other end. This will help you avoid tangling up your yarns or having them get tangled up together if they are too long or heavy.

- Consider using foam boards whenever you are working on a big project. They are lightweight, so they can be moved around easily, and they can be used to hold down your work without damaging it or interfering with your Macramé designs or patterns. They can also be used as an anchor for any yarn that is being stressed too much by the weight of the finished project.

A large tapestry can be a wonderful thing. Use care when dealing with large tapestries. Make sure you are prepared for whatever problems or surprises might come your way. If you are not, you are likely to get yourself into trouble that might cost you hours of time and effort. But my experience tells me that never giving up is the best thing to do!

CHAPTER 6

THE FRAYING

What is Fraying?

As the pieces of your Macramé project unravel, the knots loosen, and pieces come loose. This strand may come undone, or your whole project may fall apart. You can share a Macramé project with a friend if you don't have the time or patience to finish it before the project falls apart.

In the following pages, we will show you how to prevent fraying and other problems that may arise during a Macramé project.

Why does Fraying happen?

There are two main reasons why fraying happens in Macramé projects: knotting too tightly when tying fringes or pulling too hard on one side of a fringe while working with it. This is because loops are weaker when made from one strand rather than three strands in a triangle formation. Knots should also be smaller to prevent breaking in case you accidentally pull on an already existing knot in the fringe.

How to Prevent Fraying?

Here are some ways to prevent fraying when knotting fringes in your Macramé projects:

- Use thicker strands when creating knots in your Macramé projects. Thicker strands are harder to break, especially if the knot is large. If the strand is too thick, it may be difficult to work with, and it will affect the size of your knot. You can make a double knot using two strands of 24-gauge wire, for example; this will make a bigger and stronger knot than one made from three strands of 24-gauge wire which only makes a single knot.

- Work on improving your knots by practicing more and working on precision when making knots in Macramé projects. This will give you better knots that will not easily unravel or break in case you accidentally pull on the fringe.

- Iron over your work. This is when you can iron your Macramé project when it is completed and still warm; this will prevent fraying.

- Keep your Macramé project warm while you work on it. When your Macramé project is completed, take off all of the excess fringes that form the fringe pattern by using scissors or a pair of pliers to cut off extra materials. You should then hand wash your Macramé project with cold water to prevent fraying.

- Use a stronger thread when knotting fringes. Thread can easily break if you pull on it too hard while knotting your Macramé project. In the past, fishermen would use a stronger thread for knotting as they knew that they would have to pull very hard on the line to catch a fish.

- Use heavier materials in your Macramé projects to prevent fraying. Heavy materials do not fray as easily as light materials because they are hard to pull on during a project. You can even double up fringe strands using heavy material such as leather or velvet cord; doing this will make knotting easier and will give smoother edges for your Macramé.

- Do not soak your Macramé project in the water while working on it. When you do this, fraying will occur because there is no time for the strand to dry. If you like, you can use a wet-dry vac to remove excess water from your Macramé project before you work on it.

- Leave your Macramé project alone while it dries; this will prevent fraying. Fraying occurs when things are left damp and become cold; if you leave your Macramé project alone for an hour or two after completing it, the edges will not fray even if they did get wet when working with them.

- Do not allow foreign materials into your Macramé projects. For example, do not put any pins in your Macramé projects because this may break the strands. When you work with Macramé, you should always use pliers to push out any hidden objects like screws or nails that may get into your project.

- Do not step on your Macramé projects while working on them; this is when you can cause fraying. If you step on your Macramé project while it is completed, the fibers will break because they are knotted together. To avoid this, please place the material down at the same spot every time you walk past it to prevent fraying.

- Use a table with a hard surface to work on; this will prevent fraying and your knots from loosening.

- Use pins to hold down your Macramé project when not in use;

this will prevent fraying and materials from falling apart.

How to Repair Fraying?

When your Macramé project is done, you may want to repair frayed edges, especially if you were not able to work on it for an extended time. For example, if you left your Macramé project unfinished for a week after completing it, the surfaces of the materials may have become frayed. In this case, you should use a seam ripper to remove frayed threads from your Macramé project and then re-knot them to prevent further fraying.

How Do You Repair Fraying From Knots?

In cases of knotting too tightly or pulling on one side of a fringe too hard while working on a Macramé project, you can repair fraying knots by using a sharp needle and a curved needle which is used for sewing leather together. Use the sharp needle first to pierce through the middle of the knot and make it loose again. Then use the curved needle to pull through the knot, making it look smoother and stronger.

Once your Macramé project is complete, you can use a wet-dry vacuum cleaner to remove excess water that may have formed on the project. You can then iron your Macramé project to dry it off; be sure to only touch the fringes with the back of your iron. This will prevent fraying on all of your knots.

If your Macramé projects are made from silk or wool, you should make sure that they are scorched before storing them away; otherwise, mold may form which is toxic if swallowed by animals.

CHAPTER 7

DYEING BY IMMERSION

The technique of dyeing by immersion is one of the ways we can dye and pattern fabric without worrying too much about getting chemical stains on our hands or clothes. Here, we will cover how to do just that using Macramé.

The Dyeing Process

First, the yarn must be soaked in the dye. Some dyers will use a dish to submerge their yarn, while others prefer to use a container of some sort to hold their yarns, with shade on the bottom. I do not recommend using a sink or washing machine unless you can get rid of the water afterward.

Second, the yarn must sit in the dye for about one hour. A good place to do this is in your kitchen since it is at least somewhat safe.

Third, you must remove all excess bits of yarn is have stuck onto itself or other objects when it dried. It is effortless for these excess bits to become permanent stains, so make sure to take the time to remove them now.

Fourth, rinse your yarn thoroughly in cold or warm water until it runs fairly clear. You must make sure there are no excess dye particles left on the yarn, as this can create splotches and unevenness when it dries.

Fifth, hang your dyed yarn outside to dry where there is a gust of air—a ceiling fan works well—and the temperature is not too high or low. You will want at least a few days to let your yarn completely dry before doing anything else with it.

Sixth, if you want the yarn to retain its color, you can place it in an airtight plastic bag and store it for several days before use. If you plan to use your colored yarn for something such as a scarf or shawl, you can simply allow it to dry out in the sun.

The technique of Macramé is used when we want to dye multiple pieces of yarn at once, and we do not want them all to run together (like in crocheting), and we also do not want them all to turn out the same (like in knitting). Macramé is a form of braiding that incorporates knots and where we use colors and patterns that make up our weaving. It is a very popular form of braiding and can be adapted into other braiding styles as well. Macramé also helps to give a soft, flexible feeling to the woven pieces.

When we use Macramé to dye our yarns, we will need a good, sturdy piece of Macramé cord. Fabric weave is only one of the many Macramé forms that can be used for dyed yarns. Macramé also lends itself well to cording and bracelets, so have fun experimenting with this enjoyable craft!

Dip-Dyed Macramé DIY Necklace

On one side, include all three end caps to a 12mm dive ring.
Like many crafting methods, it makes more sense the more you do it. With some practice, you will be able to produce a flexible, attractive Macramé DIY device.

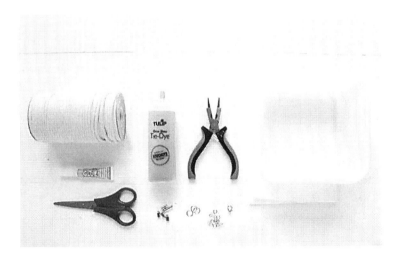

Cut three hairs of Macramé rope, determining at least 36 inches each.

Position the hairs of rope on a flat surface area, side by side. Discover the middle point of the rope trio and take a psychological note.

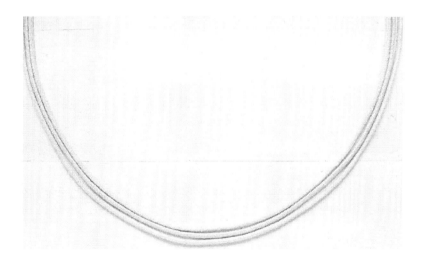

Take the best end of the rope and locate it below itself.

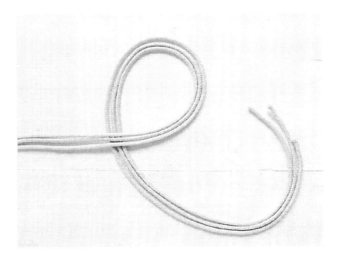

Bring completion of the rope up.

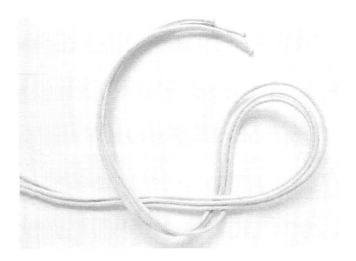

Location completion beneath the loop and directly through.

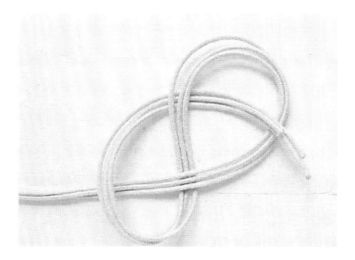

Pull carefully. This develops a single completed knot.

Now, itis time to deal with the left side. Bring the other end over the rope, positioning it near the knot your simply produced.

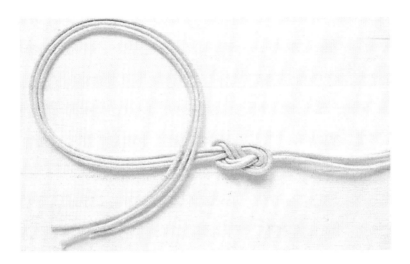

Bring completion beneath the rope and up.

Place completion through the loop, positioning it over, then under, and directly through.

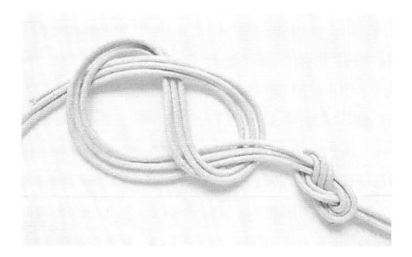

Pull carefully to finish the 2nd knot. Reverse the knot and re-position till you have attained your wanted appearance if required.

Trim completions of the rope.

You can dip color the knots or the whole piece. It's completely as much as you!

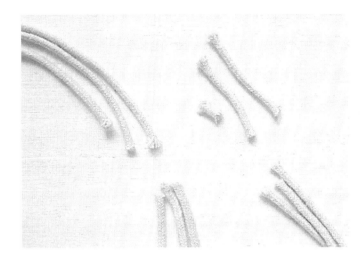

Location of the Macramé DIY cable inside the container.

Under running water, wash the rope till the water turns clear. Set out to dry entirely.

Optional: For additional information, include three 7mm dive rings to each hair of rope. Utilize the flattening part of the pliers to protect each dive ring.

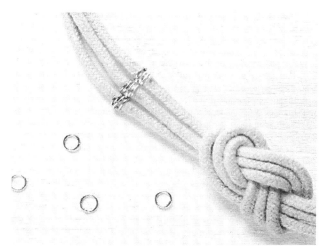

Glue 5mm end caps to the ends of the rope. Delegate dry.

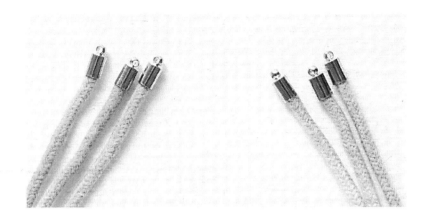

Take the Macramé pattern. Fortunately, you do not require to be a Macramé pro to take on this dip-dyed Macramé DIY pendant. With a couple of creative knots and standard natural Macramé cables, you can accept the pattern in your closet.

DIY Dyed Macramé Backdrop

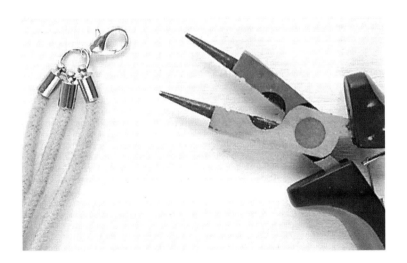

- First things initially, I bought two pattern sheets from Etsy to get this piece began; I had never produced a Macramé piece before so desired to make certain I wasn't winging it (a minimum of for a start anyhow), for the middle area I followed the guidelines here, and for the two either side of that I followed these directions, naturally if you'd choose to switch out the middle three areas for a YouTube tutorial then you absolutely can! I simply wished to ensure I was doing it properly to start with.

- You will wish to get your rope all set for the middle area initially, as we are going to begin at the center then work our escape for this task. I cut sixteen 20-foot cables of rope; in hindsight, this was somewhat too long; however, I would rather it be too long than too brief. To connect them to your wood rod, you require to fold each piece of rope in half and install them to the bar utilizing the Larks Head Knot method.

- I simply made up the next areas on either side of these; however, it was VERY simple; it's merely a cross between the first tutorial and the 2nd. I began by cutting ten pieces of rope overall, then connecting them on as constantly with a Larks Head Knot. Repeat this with ten more pieces of rope on the other side.

- Now all that's left to do is cut the Macramé to the length you prefer; I chose to cut each piece separately in angles at the bottom to develop a great rugged line style. It assists in getting a ruler and marking the two outdoor pieces of rope on that area (these will be the fastest), then cut at a diagonal angle to the center of that piece and repeat on the other side.

- Next, tape up completions of each of the ropes so that completions do not fray when you are dealing with the rope, then you are going to wish to take your hand and one piece of string and begin wrapping the rope around and around up until you've gathered a big part of it, then protect with a rubber band. This simply makes dealing with the long yarn a lot simpler rather than needing to thread and weave extremely long hairs! Ok, so now you are all set to either follow the actions in this book to develop the very same main pattern as me or pick a various Macramé piece.

- Next, it is time to begin on the two areas on either side of the middle (one at a time), you will wish to cut twelve 20-foot cables of ropes for each, and then again install them to the rod utilizing the Larks Head method. This specific pattern utilizes the Diagonal Clove Hitch strategy.

- Keep going till you've ended up passing away the whole ends of each area, do not stress if the color is beginning to approach the rope a little, that's completely regular, plus it makes a genuinely gorgeous faded result!

CHAPTER 8

KNOTS

Main Knots Used
Square/Reef Knot

This is the primary knot used. This is done by binding the line or rope around a certain object. It is also known as the base knot. You could make it by tying a left hand over a knot over a right hand. In short, right over left, and left it over right.

Half Hitch

This is done by working the end of one line over the standing part of the knot. It is one of the most valuable components of knots, bends, and hitches, among anything else.

Overhand Knot

Another knot you could use is the overhand knot. It is known as one of the world's fundamental stitches and is especially helpful in Macramé. To tie, you could simply loop a thread to the end with the help of your thumb. Or, you could also twist a bight by placing your hand over your wrist as you loop. Use your fingers to work to the end.

Other Knots
Capuchin Knot

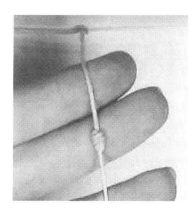

This is a great beginning knot and can be used as the foundation for the base of the project. Use a lightweight cord for this—it can be purchased at craft stores or online, wherever you get your Macramé supplies.

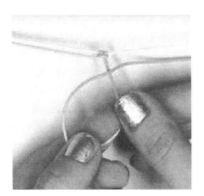

Observe the photos as you move along with this project, and take your time to make sure you are using the right string at the right point of the project. Don't rush, and make sure you have even tension throughout. Practice makes perfect, but with the illustrations to help you, you will find it is not hard at all to create.

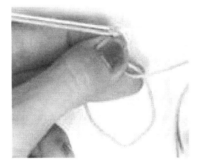

Start with the base cord, tie the knot onto this, and work your way along with the project.

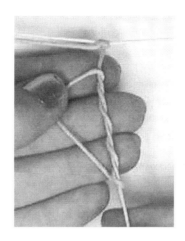

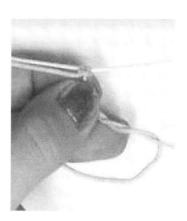

Twist the cord around itself 2 times, pulling the string through the center to form the knot.

For the finished project, make sure that you have all your knots secure and firm throughout, and do your best to make sure it is all even. It is going to take practice before you can get it perfectly each time, but remember that practice does make perfect, and with time, you are going to get it without too much trouble.
Make sure all is even and secure and tie off. Snip off all the loose ends, and you are ready to go!

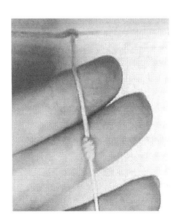

Crown Knot

It can be used as the foundation for the base of the project. Use a lightweight cord for this—it can be purchased at craft stores or online, wherever you get your Macramé supplies.

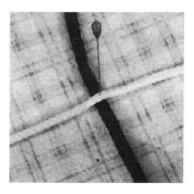

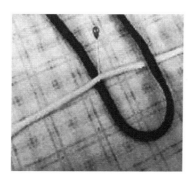

Use a pin to help keep everything in place as you are working.

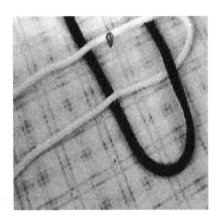

Weave the strings in and out of each other, as you can see in the photos. It helps to practice with different colors to help you see what is going on.

Pull the knot tight, then repeat for the next row on the outside.

Continue to do this as often as you like to create the knot. You can make it as thick as you like, depending on the project. You can also create more than one length on the same cord.

For the finished project, make sure that you have all your knots secure and firm throughout, and make sure it is all even. It is going to take practice before you can get it ideally each time, but remember that practice does make perfect, and with time, you are going to get it without too much trouble.

Make sure all is even and secure and tie off. Snip off all the loose ends, and you are ready to go!

Diagonal Double Half Knot

This is a great knot to use for basket hangings, decorations, or any projects that are going to require you to put weight on the project. Use a heavier weight cord for this, which you can find at craft stores or online.

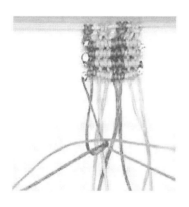

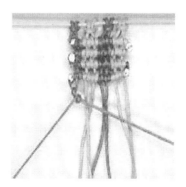

Start at the top of the project and work your way toward the bottom. Keep it even as you work your way throughout the piece. Tie the knots at 4-inch intervals, working your way down the entire thing.

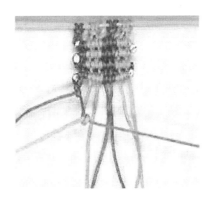

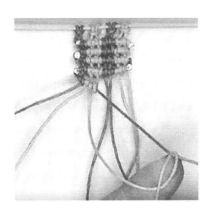

Weave in and out throughout, watching the photo, as you can see for the right placement of the knots. Again, it helps to practice with different colors so you can see what you need to do throughout the piece.

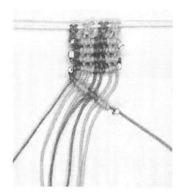

For the finished project, make sure that you have all your knots secure and firm throughout, and make sure it is all even. It is going to take practice before you can get it perfectly each time, but remember that practice does make perfect, and with time, you are going to get it without too much trouble.

Make sure all is even and secure and tie off. Snip off all the loose ends, and you are ready to go!

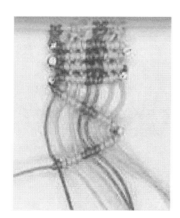

Frivolity Knot

Use a lightweight cord for this—it can be purchased at craft stores or online, wherever you get your Macramé supplies.

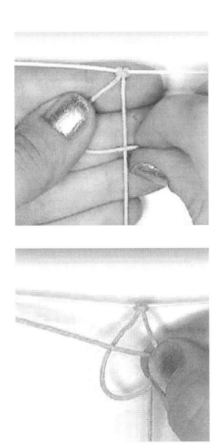

Use the base string as the guide to hold it in place, then tie the knot onto this. This is a very straightforward knot; watch the photo and follow the directions you see.

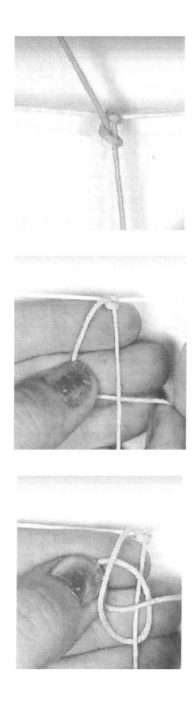

Pull the end of the cord up and through the center.

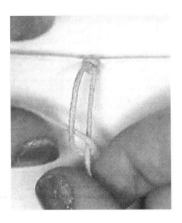

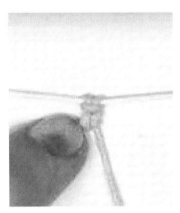

For the finished project, make sure that you have all your knots secure and firm throughout, and make sure it is all even. It is going to take practice before you can get it ideally each time, but remember that practice does make perfect, and with time, you are going to get it without too much trouble.
Make sure all is even and secure and tie off. Snip off all the loose ends, and you are ready to go!

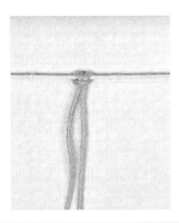

Horizontal Double Half Knot

Use a lightweight cord for this—it can be purchased at craft stores or online, wherever you get your Macramé supplies.

Start at the top of the project and work your way toward the bottom. Keep it even as you work your way throughout the piece. Tie the knots at 4-inch intervals, working your way down the entire thing.

For the finished project, make sure that you have all your knots secure and firm throughout, and make sure it is all even. It is going to take practice before you can get it ideally each time, but remember that practice does make perfect, and with time, you are going to get it without too much trouble.
Make sure all is even and secure and tie off. Snip off all the loose ends, and you are ready to go!

Josephine Knot

This is a good knot to use for basket hangings, decorations, or any projects that are going to require you to put weight on the project. Use a heavier weight cord for this, which you can find at craft stores or online.

Watch the photos very carefully as you move along with this project, and take your time to make sure you are using the right string at the right point of the project.

Use the pins along with the knots that you are tying, and work with more extensive areas all at the same time. This is going to help you keep the project in place as you continue to work throughout the piece.

Pull the ends of the knots through the loops, and form the ring in the center of the strings.

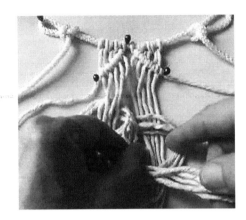

For the finished project, make sure that you have all your knots secure and firm throughout, and make sure it is all even. It is going to take practice before you can get it perfectly each time, but remember that practice does make perfect, and with time, you are going to get it without too much trouble.

Make sure all is even and secure, and tie off. Snip off all the loose ends, and you are ready to go!

Lark's Head Knot

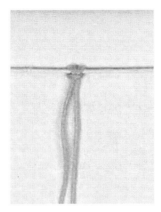

This is a great beginning knot for any project and can be used as the foundation for the base of the project. Use a lightweight cord for this—it can be purchased at craft stores or online, wherever you get your Macramé supplies.

Use the base string as the core part of the knot, working around the end of the string with the cord. Make sure all is even as you loop the string around the base of the cord.

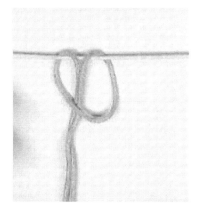

Create a slip knot around the base of the string and keep both ends even as you pull the cord through the center of the piece.

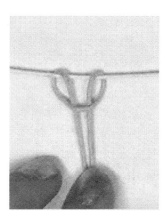

For the finished project, make sure that you have all your knots secure and firm throughout, and make sure it is all even. It is going to take practice before you can get it ideally each time, but remember that practice does make perfect, and with time, you are going to get it without too much trouble.
Make sure all is even and secure and tie off. Snip off all the loose ends, and you are ready to go!

The Wrapped Knot

A vintage knot technique, the wrapped knot is seen frequently in plant hangers made from Macramé. The process of making a Wrapped Knot is called lashing in some vintage textile crafts. The wrapped knot is used for securing the bundle of numerous cords that require being grouped. To finish the wrapped knot, cut off the bottom and top ends of the working cord. The wrapped knot is closely related to another pattern known as the linen stitch.

The wrapped knot may be used for bracelets, necklaces, the branches of tree decorations. Getting the knots long is quite challenging and it difficult for practical decorative purposes; as such, it is usually an amazing challenge to use the wrapped to execute real Macramé projects. Creating the wrapped knots requires a minimum of three cords for holding the knots. The material for the working cord is separate and measures a minimum of 30 inches in length. The knot itself must measure between 1 and 2 inches.

Method

Vertically arrange the cords that hold the knot. At the end of the working cord, tie an overhand knot. Secure this knot to the other cords, on their left. Determine the area to be wrapped and fold the working line a little beyond this area. Bring the other end of the working cord back to the direction of the knot. Proceed to secure the area folded.

Now, wrap the returning working end around the holding cords, allowing it to pass beneath the tight end. Tug it to the left gently.

Again, wrap the returning end around the holding cord as described above, making the second wrap snug close to the first wrap; under the first wrap. Continue this until you have covered the desired area, leaving the folded end of the working cord in a loop. Slot the end of the working cord into the loop and pull it all through. Ensure to hold the bundle tight while doing this.

At the other end, tug the secured end just at the top. This would pull the folded area in and, with it, the working end. Keep pulling the tight end until the cord goes about halfway through the knot.

Cut the bottom and top end of the working cord off at the ends of the knot. If it is only practicing and you would like to reuse your cord, however, you can skip cutting the ends off.

The Barrel Knot

This knot is often used in Macramé projects, most for securing knots at the end as a finish or just to hold the knot from loosening. It is, however, also handy for firm knots. The Barrel Knot has been in existence for a long time, as evidenced by references made to this handy knot in Macramé literature.

Basic Design

The basic design is the more commonly used Barrel knot and is considered as the standard of Barrel knots. A minimum of fifteen inches length of the cord is required to practice this knot.

Fasten the cord to the right part of the board. Create a loop by moving the working end anti-clockwise. In the end, allow it to lay vertically.

From below the certain part, roll the working end over the secured part, moving leftward and inward of the loop.

Do this a second time, the new roll on the left of the old. Snug both wraps closely together without overlap.

Tighten the knot slowly to make it firm and secure, and make sure you avoid any form of twisting or curls in the knot. To achieve the best results, take your time to make cords taut to avoid any slacks in the wraps. You can then tug the secured end slowly to make the loop tight.

The spiral knot is a collection of square knots. Repeating the square knots onto the same cord creates a spiral pattern. Spiral knots are combined with other knots to create a variety of patterns in the hanger.

Steps

Take the left working cord and place it on the holding cords.

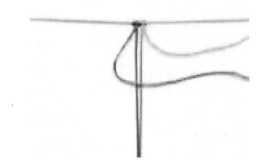

Next, take the right working cord over that, pass it under the holding cord, and bring it up through the loop on the other side, which was created by passing the left working cord on the right.

Pull the cords from either side tightly to create the first half of the square knot.
Repeat the above-mentioned steps to create a full square knot. But, make sure that you always start with the working cord from the same side with

which you initially started.

Keep repeating the steps to tie several square knots to create a spiral pattern.

CHAPTER 9

PATTERNS

Macramé is an ancient technique of knotting, weaving, and braiding plant materials like cords, twigs, or grass into the fabric. There are many variations on this technique that involve creating different patterns (much like knitting or crochet) using knots of various types.

This will introduce you to some basic patterns and get you started creating your Macramé projects.

Arrow Pattern

This pattern is an easy-to-learn Macramé pattern. It is a good choice for beginners working on Macramé projects that might be a bit more vertical, such as a wall hanging or vertical basket.

Steps in Doing the Arrows Pattern

- Find two sticks that are approximately the same length. If you don't have two sticks of the same length, use pieces of wood to create a third piece.

- Put one stick in the middle and tie a knot underneath it. Be sure to leave enough string on the ends so that you will be able to use them as additional ties when working on your pattern.

- Take both ends and weave them under and over each other about 2-3 times, then take both ends and weave them under and over each other once again.

- Take the first ends, twirl them around the stick, and bring them out.

- Take both ends and weave them under and over each other once randomly.

- Repeat step 4 randomly again to create a similar effect to step 5.

- Do steps 3-6 three more times, creating a total of five patterns on the original piece of string/stick/wood/etc. which you will use as your template to create the rest of the pattern

- Once you have completed all five patterns on your knot template, attach one end to the middle stick. Continue adding rotated patterns until you reach the other end.

- Once you reach the other end, tie a knot (redoing this step will ensure that the pattern is symmetrical).

- Complete any remaining necessary tying steps (tying ends, knotting ends).

Fishbone Pattern

This pattern was often used in tribal or traditional clothing from other countries. It is simple to make and has a unique pattern that can add a lot to a piece of clothing.

Steps in Doing the Fishbone Pattern

- Find two sticks of the same size and shape (one will form the backbone; one will form the dorsal fin). Tie knots underneath both sticks at their ends, so they can stay in place.

- Take both ends and weave them over and under each other about two times, then take both ends and weave them over and under each other once again.

- Take the first ends, twirl them around the sticks, and bring them out.

- Take both ends and weave them under and over each other one time randomly.

- Repeat step 4 randomly again to create a similar effect to step 4.

- Repeat steps 4-5 once more to create a total of three patterns on the original sticks.

- Tie two knots on either side of the sticks, one at the top of the stick facing down and another at the bottom on the other side facing up to face each other.

- Take both ends and weave them over and under each other one time randomly so that the two middle pieces are connecting.

- Tie a knot directly in-between the two pieces.

- Complete any remaining necessary tying steps (tying ends, knotting ends).

Butterfly Pattern

This is a very common and easy pattern that can be made using any type of plant material. It is often used to add simple decoration to Macramé pieces, such as tying grass braids, finishing braids, or spacing pieces.

Steps in Doing the Butterfly Pattern

- Find a piece of string/stick/wood, etc. that is approximately the same length as your template. If you don't have two sticks that are the same length, use pieces of wood or different sizes to create a third piece that is just about as long as your original template.

- Put one stick in the middle and tie a knot underneath it. Be sure to leave enough string on the ends so that you will be able to use them as additional ties when working on your pattern.

- Take both ends and weave them over and under each other one time randomly.

- Take the first end, twirl it around the stick, and bring it out.

- Take both ends and weave them over and under each other randomly so that they face in different directions.

- Repeat step 5 twice more to create a total of three patterns on your knot template (one for each side of the stick).

- Complete any necessary tying steps (tying ends, knotting ends).

Leaves Pattern

This is a variation of the fishbone pattern that is easy to follow and create. A good choice for beginners working on Macramé projects that might be a bit more horizontal, such as a wall hanging or basket.

Steps in Doing the Leaves Pattern

- Find two sticks the same size and shape (one will form the backbone; one will form the leaves). Tie knots underneath both sticks at their ends, so they can stay in place.

- Take both ends and weave them over and under each other one time randomly.

- Take the first ends, twirl them around the sticks, and bring them out.

- Take both ends and weave them over and under each other randomly so that they face in different directions.

- Repeat step 4 two more times to create a total of three patterns on your original sticks.

- Complete any necessary tying steps (tying ends, knotting ends).

- Once you have completed steps 1-6 on your stitch template, tie one end to another end directly under one of the middle patterns you created earlier. Do this by taking both ends and weaving them over and under each other once again randomly so that they are facing in different directions.

- Loop the second end around the first and tie a knot directly in-between the two pieces.

- Complete any remaining necessary tying steps (tying ends, knotting ends).

Triangles Pattern

This is a variation of the Leaves Pattern that is easy to follow and create. A good choice for beginners working on Macramé projects that might be a bit more horizontal, such as wall hangings or baskets.

Steps in Doing the Triangles Pattern

- Find two sticks of the same size and shape (one will form the backbone; one will form a triangle). Tie knots underneath both sticks at their ends, so they can stay in place. Be sure to leave enough string so that you will be able to use it as an additional tie.

- Take both ends and weave them over and under each other one time randomly.
- Take the first end, twirl it around the stick, and bring it out.

- Take both ends and weave them under and over each other once again, this time in an upside-down triangle pattern.

- Repeat step 4 two times more to create a total of three patterns on your original sticks.

- Complete any necessary tying steps (tying ends, knotting ends).

- Once you have completed steps 1-6 on your stitch template, tie one en to another directly under one of the middle patterns you created earlier in the same way you tied them in step 6.

- Repeat steps 7 and 8 on the other side of your original sticks.

- Complete any necessary tying steps (tying ends, knotting ends).

Net Pattern

- This is a variation of the fishbone pattern that is easy to follow and create. A good choice for beginners working on Macramé projects that might be a bit more horizontal, such as a wall hanging or basket.

Steps in Doing the Net Pattern

- Find two sticks of the same size, shape, and length (one will form the backbone and the net). Tie knots underneath both posts at their ends, so they can stay in place.

- Take both ends and weave them over and under each other one time randomly.

- Take both ends and weave them over and under each other once again, this time in an upside-down triangle pattern.

- Repeat steps 2-3 six more times to create a total of seven patterns on your original sticks.

- Complete any necessary tying steps (tying ends, knotting ends).

- Take the first end, twirl it around the stick, and bring it out.

- Take both ends and weave them over and under each other randomly so that they face in different directions. This is where the second end will be tied to the first end later on in step 9.

- Repeat step 7 on the other side of your original sticks.

- Complete any necessary tying steps (tying ends, knotting ends).

Picot Net Pattern

- This is a variation of the net pattern that is easy to follow and create. A good choice for beginners working on Macramé projects that might be a bit more horizontal, such as wall hangings or baskets.

Steps in Doing the Picot Net Pattern

- Find two sticks of the same size, shape, and length (one will form the backbone and the net). Tie knots underneath both sticks at their ends, so they can stay in place.

- Take both ends and weave them over and under each other one time randomly.

- Take both ends and weave them over and under each other once again, this time in an upside-down triangle pattern. You may also notice that the pattern is very similar to the fishbone pattern.

- Repeat steps 2-3 seven more times to create a total of eight patterns on your original sticks.

- Complete any necessary tying steps (tying ends, knotting ends).

- Once you have completed steps 1-5 on your stitch template, tie one end to another directly under one of the middle patterns you created earlier in the same way you tied them in step 6.

- Complete any necessary tying steps (tying ends, knotting ends).

- Take the second end you left long in step 1 and tie it to the second end on the other side of your original sticks in the same fashion as you did with your first end.

- Complete any remaining necessary tying steps (tying ends, knotting ends).

CHAPTER 10

PROJECTS

Beginners Projects

Macramé Bracelet Patterns

If initially only strands were used in making Macramé jewelry, now craftsmen add absolutely all accessories to their work based on their imagination: ribbons, beads, cabochons, buckles, and more.

Also, jewelry using the Macramé technique can find such defining words as micro-Macramé. The difference between a micro-Macramé and a macro is that only the finest threads are used for the micro-Macramé, and the workflow becomes more tedious, and the difference is visible to the naked eye.

One of the first Macramé embellishments is the bright and colorful friendship bracelets, many known as mouline threads.

Now we will show modern Macramé ideas that can be found in any type of jewelry: earrings, necklaces, pendants, and bracelets.

A master class of bracelets made of string and beads using the Macramé technique.

Materials:

- Nylon or wax cable

- Beads green, orange, blue, yellow

- Scissors

Directions:

- Prepare seven pieces of ribbon, 100 cm in length, assemble and bind at the top into a knot. The outer cable is slightly offset, it will be the lead cable, which we will tie the rest.

- We take the next rope and first draw it on top of the lead cable, turn it over, tuck it under the lead cable, and put it in the loop. Now we bring it back to the lead cable, draw it on top, rotate it, pull it under the lead cable, and put it in the formed loop.

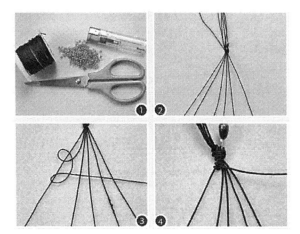

- Now we tie the lead cable in the same way, with each other (Fig. 5).

- After that, we place the lead cable on top of all the wires in the row and start the binding again, but from below. (Fig. 6-7)

- Turn the lead cable again and attach the wires to it. (Fig. 8)

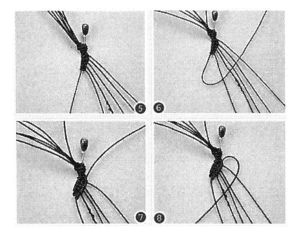

- Once again, we connect the lead cable to all cables. (Fig. 9)

- Now we inscribe each cable except the leading beads in the order as in photo no. 10th.

- Then we place the lead tape on the ribbons after the beads and the ribbons are made three times. (Fig. 11, 12, and 13)

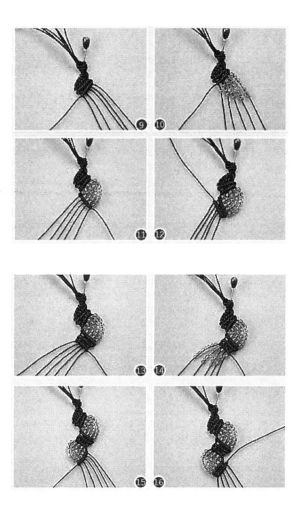

- When the desired length is woven, straighten the ends of the cables with scissors and lay them parallel to each other. (Fig. 20)

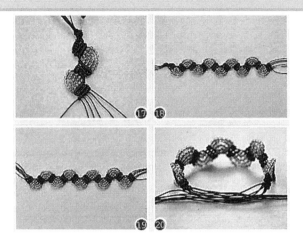

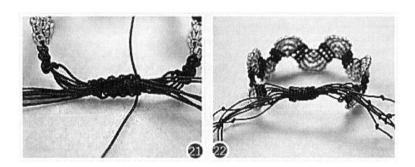

- We decorate the bracelet lock in the form of Shambhala knots.

- At the same time, we tie each edge of the lace into a knot.

The bracelet is ready!

Sunscreen Macramé Holder

Materials:

- Cord

- Forklift

- sunscreen

- Thin, empty flask

- Bookmark

- Clippers

- Flash candle

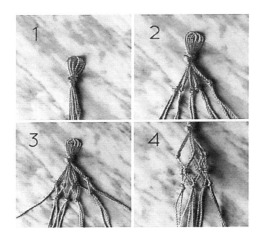

Directions:

- Cut five-string bits, about 20" long.

- Fold in half and tie the center of one big sweater. Tape down the knot to stay in place.

- Divide the string into five pairs and knot each couple down to around 1". Take another 1" down, take one line, and knot it from the pair next to it with a loop.

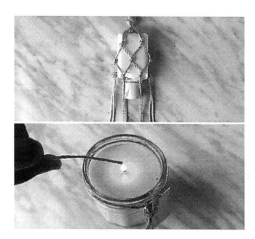

- Continue to cover the length of the bottle for about four rows of knots. Slide your bottle in to test the fit and the appropriate number of knots. For ease of use, I put the bottle on the cap side downwards.

- If the fit is right, tie the first knot to keep the bottle in place with all the threads.

- Place each string over a candle, overheat to melt the ends, and avoid fraying.

- Add a carabiner (or keyring) to the top knot to finish off, and connect to your pocket.

- The travel size bottle last year was enough for us all summer, but you can replenish it as desired. You don't need to dig in your pocket now anytime you need a drop of sunscreen.

Feathers

Charms and feathers always look cool. They just add a lot of that enchanting feeling to your house, and knowing that you could make Macramé décor with charms and feathers takes your crafting game to new heights! Check out the instructions below and try it out for yourself!

Materials:

- Stick/dowel

- Feathers and charms with holes (for you to insert the thread in)

- Embroidery/laundry rope (or any other rope or thread that you want)

Directions:

- Cut as many pieces of rope as you want. Around 10 to 12 pieces are good, and then fold each in half. Make sure to create a loop at each end, like the ones you see below:

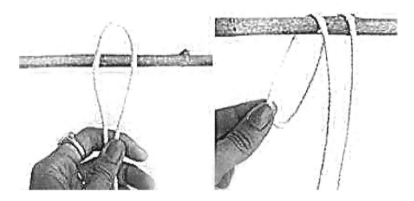

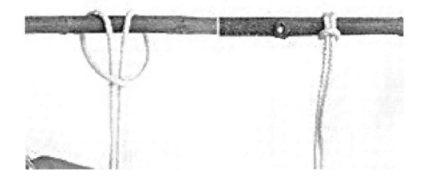

- Then, go and loop each piece of thread on the stick.

- Make use of the square knot and make sure you have four strands for each knot. Let the leftmost strand cross the two strands, and then put it over the strands that you have in the middle. Tuck it under the middle two, as well.

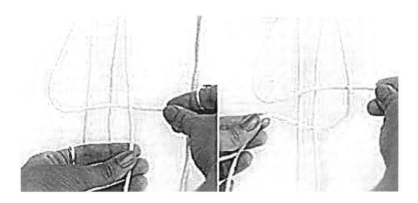

Check under the strands and let the rightmost strand be tucked under the loop to the left-hand strand.

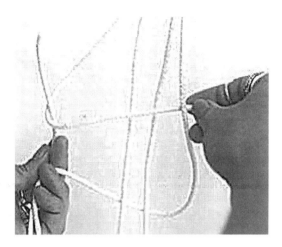

- Tighten the loop by pulling the outer strands together and start with the left to repeat the process on the four strands. You will then see that a square knot has formed after tightening the loops together.

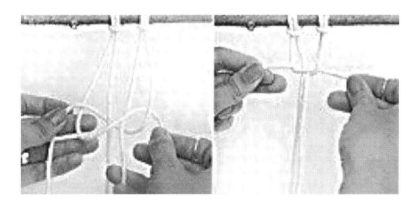

- Connect the strands by doing square knots with the remaining four pieces of rope and then repeat the process from the left side. Tighten the loop by pulling the outer strands together and start with the left to repeat the process on the four strands. You will then see that a square knot has formed after the loops have been tightened together.

- You can then do eight knots and then just attach charms and feathers to the end. Glue them in and burn the ends for better effect!

Pom Pom Hanging Macramé

Materials:

- Cord Macramé

- Fabric

- Scissors

- Macramé 4-inch net

- Small pan

- The measure of tape (optional)

- Pompom (optional) maker

Directions:

- Cut 8 bits of a 7-foot-long Macramé chain.

- Thread through the Macramé hoop all 8 bits, and line up the ends.

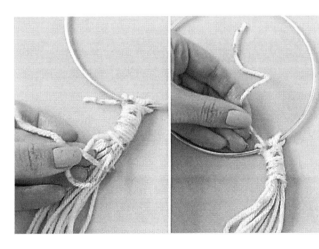

- Pull out about 24 inches of a piece of thread. Hold the end at the tip of the hoop and circle the bottom upwards.

- Wrap the yarn firmly around both of the Macramé bits and on top of the thread, leaving the string that you've just made clear. Cover before you reach the perfect length, then you are almost out of yarn.

- Thread the end into the circle and pull it up on top of the strand. This will draw the loop upwards and protect the cover. Trim the leftover thread.

- Separate the threads into 4 parts.

- Allow the first knot about 8 inches deep. Using a square knot. To ensure that every segment is even (recommended), you may either observe the marks or use a tape measure/ruler.

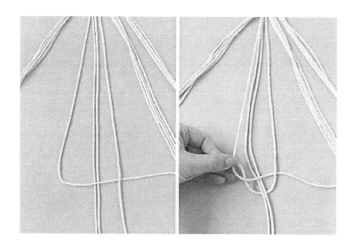

- I continue on the left (but that is perfect on either side). To make the square knot, cross the left side over the two middle sides, just under the top. Drag the right side under the middle strands and through the circle forward.

- Repeat to the right leg. That creates one knot in the square. Repeat on any group of strands five times, measuring as appropriate, so they are all equal.

- The fibers split. To build the next series of knots, take two from the right knot and two from the left.

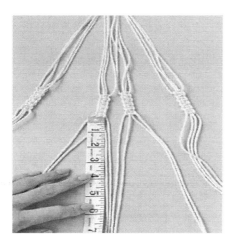

- Measure another 5 inches down (give the larger pot more space) and make another 5 square knots. Repeat, removing individual group lines. Ultimately, you will need to hand over the job to solve all the knots.

- Now, make six pompoms!

- Add one pompom to the top of the hanger by knotting and winding it around. Add then four pompoms to the first row of Macramé knots by wrapping and knotting around the center ends.

- Place the pot in between the knots' second row so that the knots rest around the pot. To keep the cup in place, repeat the tie knot from the top of the hanger.

- Then, tie a pompom to the bottom of the hanger and remove the excess string, so they are all even, around 6 inches in length. Unravel stops as you want to.

- It is ready to sit now! Fill the pot and put the Macramé planter back inside. Screw a hook securely into the wall, then loop the net around the planter.

- Fill the pot inside the Macramé planter and put it back. Screw a hook securely into the wall, then loop the net around the planter.

Keychain Heart

Materials:

- 8 smaller beads

- One big bead

- 8 threads, each 27 inches long.

Directions:

- You will be making an overhand knot. Take one thread, fold it in half, now form a loop on top of the folded thread. This can be done by using your thumb as a guide to how long the loop should be. Then hold the thread at this length so that the loop is isolated.

- While keeping the loop isolated, create another loop with the rest of the thread and then place the original loop through the new loop while keeping hold of the original circle, and then when through, you can pull to tighten. You should end up with something like the picture below.

- This is what your overhand knot should look like.

- Take another thread, place it over your prior thread with the knot in it ensuring that the knot is in the middle of the new thread you have just chosen.

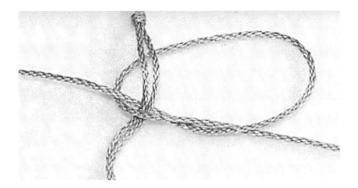

- Now you will tie a square knot. Take the left-hand side of the thread that you have just laid down (the one without the knot) and place it over the line above it and under the thread on the right. Then take the right-side thread and thread it under the thread at the bottom and under the left-hand side, and through the loop that the left-hand thread has created. Simultaneously, pull the lines on the left and right side so that it tightens, and a knot is created.

- Take the single thread on the right, place it over the two threads in the middle and under the left thread. Now take the left line under the two threads in the middle and under the loop created on the right. Pull to tighten (both sides at the same time) and create your knot.

- Take the single thread on the left, then take the single thread on the right. Ensure that both threads are horizontal. For now, you will only be working with the right, so you can set the left side down until later.

- Take a new single thread, fold it in half, make sure there is a loop created at the top. Then place the line behind the single thread on the right and fold over the top. Now, pull the two loose threads through the middle of the loop so that it looks as above. Then, pull the threads so that the line tightens, and you will end up with a Lark's Head knot.

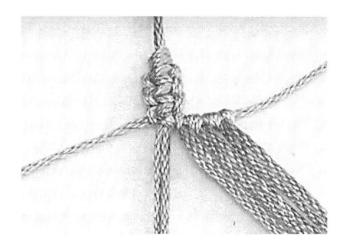

- Take two more single threads and repeat step 7 until you end up with two more Lark's Head knots on the right.

- Take the left single thread, which should be horizontal, as stated earlier. Then create three more Lark's Head knots on the left single thread. It should look like the picture above.

- Now you should have three Lark's Head knots on each side.

- You should now have two threads in the middle. Take a small bead and thread it onto the two threads.

- Take a big bead and place it on the same thread pushing it to the top so that your Macramé piece looks like the one in the picture.

- Take a pair of scissors and cut the loose thread at the end of the knot leaving just the knot.

- Refer to the image above.

- From your left group of threads, take the first on the right and place it horizontally across the other threads in the bunch. Then take the thread next to it, loop it over the horizontal thread, under itself, then using the same thread loop it over the flat thread again, and finally, through the loop created. Pull to secure the knot tightly. You will have a half hitch knot.

- Repeat this step with each thread until all your threads on the left have been done.

- Take the next thread, directly under the half hitch knot, on the right. Pull this thread across horizontally and repeat the process of creating the half hitch knot.

- Repeat this process 6 more times, so you have 8 half hitch knots in total like the picture below. (Excluding the one at the bottom)

- Here you will be creating the knot at the bottom of the left side.

- Take the first thread on the right of the bottom knot. Then take the thread next to it, loop it over the horizontal thread, under itself, then, using the same thread, loop it over the flat thread again and finally through the loop created. Pull to secure the knot tightly. You will have a half hitch knot.

- Take the thread used to create the half hitch knot and place it around both horizontal threads, under itself, then, using the same threads, loop them over the flat threads and finally through the loop created. Pull to tighten.

- Then take the thread just used for the horizontal thread and place it across the remaining threads. You should have three horizontal threads. Take the threads next to it and wrap them around the three horizontal threads to create a half hitch knot. Take the next thread and wrap it around both flat lines, under itself, then using the same threads loop them over the flat lines, and finally through the loop created. Pull to tighten.

- Repeat this process, add one thread each time until you get to the last thread. Your Macramé piece should look like the image above. This is what your finished left side should look like. If you have made any mistakes, it is okay to go back and change them. The last half hitch knot can be hard to follow, but use the pictures to aid you, and you will succeed.

- For the completion of the right side, start in the same way you did for the left side. This is the same process, and if you completed the left side, you shouldn't find it too hard. Repeat the steps given earlier.

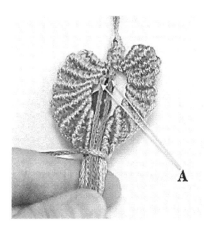

A

- When completed, it should look like the illustration given above. Don't worry if you don't get it the first time. You can always undo your stitching and try again.

- With the hanging threads from both the left and right sides, pull to make sure they are vertical. The cables should be together as one group.

- Cut a piece of the thread, around 4 inches, and fold it in half to use. Now place this piece of thread in the middle of the bunch but sitting on the top and the two ends facing the top as in the picture (thread A).

- Take a single thread from the group of threads. Wrap it around the group of threads as shown above.

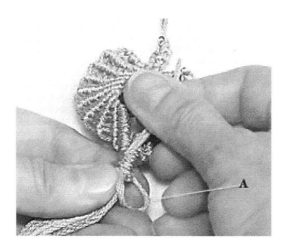

- Continue to wrap the thread around the group of threads until there is only a short portion of the single thread left. There should have been a loop created by the short piece of thread cut earlier (thread "A" in photo). Place the end of the thread (A) through the loop as shown, pull the two ends of the loose line (A) at the top so that the loose thread (A) will come out ultimately. The end of the single thread becomes trapped inside the loop creating a knot.

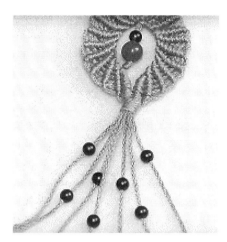

- You should have several threads hanging loose from the knot just created. Place a small bead through each thread and show them to have the same intervals between them. They should be staggered, creating the pattern shown.

- Now do an overhand knot at the end of each bead to secure it in place. Refer to earlier instructions on how to complete this.

- Trim the remaining threads from underneath the knots.

Dreamcatcher

This fantastical Macramé design is best to make that somebody distinctive to your soul as a present.

Materials:

- Single 4 inches ring of brass

- 6 meters of all strings, thickness 2 millimeters

- Fifteen Pony Beads

- Feathers

Directions:

- Bind one closure of the wire to the band of the brass.

- Cycle the wire across the ring and firmly drag it after every circuit. To begin the following line of the network, precisely coil the string about the first string. Proceed to loop until the expansion is the required shape in the core.

- You can append the beads elsewhere in the layout while attempting to make the hair clip. Shortly before inserting the bead, wrap the string and then move the string into the bead. The bead is then secured within the layout web.

- Once the web is done, you can handle the ring with the string. Lock a ring edge with a dual knot. Roll the ring's size with the strap and then paste the ends to be secured.

- Put a slice of wire, which is six to eight inches in length. Append the beads anywhere, make sure you integrate a dual knot since the last bead. Move a plumb via the beads until it becomes snug. Connect the strap to the circle with a twin knot.

- Choose an upper six-inch string perched on top of the dream catcher to hold the final piece.

DIY Macramé Bottle Hanger

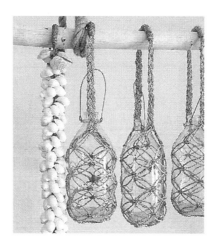

Materials:

• The Jars

• Macramé Cording

• Scissors

Do you have five minutes? That is exactly what will be needed.
One thing to bear in mind, which might seem obvious, but we will mention it anyway: We will clean our yogurt bottles and delete the stickers. Though our goo is securely stored, we are planning to use a little nice to get rid of all the sticker remnants.
"Troubles of renovation."

Directions:

- Weigh the cords. It can be as short or as long as you want. Here is the exact formula we used, which we found on Pinterest.'

Hanger length multiplied by two + jar length multiplied by ten inches We are going to go for 18 inches for the length of our hanger, so we double-checked it with String, then applied it to the height of our container attached about 10 inches and cut our String there.

We will see that this duration is much more than enough.

- After you've cut the first bit of ribbon, cut three more of the same size for a total of four pieces of the same thread.

- The cords are bent in half. Tie a knot in the upper portion of the fold. This would be the cute tiny hanger portion. Tidy up the knot by pulling on the strings until it is straight and tidy.

- Tie it around a doorknob, cabinet knob, or other items. We found it much easier to tie the knots when it was hanging.

- Take two cords and tie a pair of knots with them. Do this for each of them before you do something else. Create knots all the way around as well.

- Right now. Taking one of those knots, two of the knots they just made, grab one rope, and tie those cords together with another knot.

Return until you have 4 knots. Assuring that they are both comparable. That is the second degree of knots, and the hanger is beginning to take shape.

Through you, this is a flashlight moment.

- Repeat the 6th step, but this time, add a third row for knots. For these tiny jars to be the finest, we will consider three lines of knots.

- Carry the little container inside and make sure it stays there. If it doesn't, make minor modifications or stretch the knots out as far as possible.

If it looks good in there, simply tie a large knot at the bottom with all the loose threads. This great knot will serve as the container hanger's foundation.

- Trim or leave the extra hang, which is mainly from the knot. Use fairy lights to fill your jar. Now is the time to put them up and feel it.

It is over.

What a beautiful pair they will be.

You should hang them from your outside umbrella. We hung them with our tree and they looked great.

These would be perfect for those friendly get-togethers you are planning. Suspend them from the rooftop in a children's space for a boho look. It would make a truly fun little night light if you had some dimmer fairy lights.

Micro Macramé Christmas Decorations

Materials:

- Cord/string Macramé

- Scissors

- Twigs

- Tape masking

- Comb or hairbrush

- To the Twig Having the Cords Attached

Directions:

- To begin, cut a small twig and tie six cords together with the Lark's Head knot. We will use a cord, but we will unwind it until we've tied it to the twig and changed it from three plies to one. Any chord must be at least 2 feet long.

- How to tie a four-phase head knot for larks to bind a Lark's Head knot, fold the rope in half, and then lay it over the top of the twig in the middle.

- Bend the loop around the back of the twig and then draw the two ends together. There is a strong attraction. Rep on all six strings.

- A little Macramé decoration with sparkle lights in a white Christmas theme.

1st Square Knot

It is time to begin the first line, 3 square knots until the strings are on the twig. Four cords connect those knots, and that the first four cords come from the left and split them.
In four steps, how and when to attach a square knot for Macramé. To create the square knot, bring it out of the upper left cord so it appears like a number 4 pattern is developing.

The first cord's ends are then tucked under a fourth cord.
Then, at the end of the 4th chord, draw up from behind the middle two chords, through the space between the 1st and 2nd cords that looks like the four.

Raise the ends of the first and fourth cords to reinforce and move the knot to the tip. It is the first half of a square knot.
At Macramé College, you will learn how to tie a square knot.

The second half of a square knot should be used in the same way but on the opposite direction. But for the "4" reversed on the right side, you can make the "4" shape for the first and fourth cords.
Then draw the first cord over the fourth.

After that, feed the first cord tail underneath the second and third cords and up through the "4" type opening.
Draw the first and fourth cords' edges together to tighten, and you will get the first square knot.

3rd row

Macramé's steps for attaching a square knot continue to work in four-cord units. Attach a different square knot and then another square knot to make 3 along the top row.

In segment two, you will just tie two square knots. To do this, start by breaking the first one into cords. The first four cords of the second square knot are in row 2, followed by another. However, it will leave another two cords uncovered. A square knot may be formed by using just the middle four cords of a line for the third line.

If you feel that you need to shift the tension, try to keep the knots evenly distributed and tightened.

4-5th row

A piece of Macramé with tiny square knots fixed to a table
For row four, replicate row two with two square knots on both sides, cutting all two strings.

For row 5, please replicate row 1 of three-square knots.

6 Row Half Knot Hitch

How do you tie a four-factor half hitch? You may finish this decoration with square knots or add a series of half hitch knots.
Do a half hitch knot with the first cord in the chain, then pull horizontally across the piece. The lead rope is going to be it.

Put the second cord behind and over a lead through the loophole you've built. Repeat the knot with the second cord in a similar manner. It is just half of a hitch.

Go down the rest of the cords, being careful not to bend the lead cord flat by drawing it horizontally over the other cords behind it.
Tighten the knots by pushing on the lead rope.

Wall Hanging DIY Bohemian Macramé Mirror

Materials:

- Cording Macramé: 4mm

- Sharp Scissors (also available at JoAnn Fabrics)

- Ring of wood: 2 inches

- Wood Beads: 25millimeters Hole Size w/10mm

- With Sharp Scissors

- Wood Beads: 25millimeters Hole Size w/10mm

Directions:

Split the 4 pieces of Macramé cord into 108-inch parts.

Mirror, mirror Larks Head Knot in Macramé.

- Fold the pieces in half and tie them all together with a Lark's Head knot in the wood ring. Closely and tightly wrap the knots around each other. Break the Lark's Head links in half and tie them together in a square knot.

Model of a square knot Macramé mirror

- Make two square knots with your hands.

- Begin by tying two square knots into two additional Lark's Head knots.

Macramé square knot in mirror

- When you begin the second square knot line, bring one of the other two square knots' edges together to form one large long square knot.

- Make seven square knots, going down either side and absolutely.

- The square knot of the Macramé keeper.

- Cut the ends of the knots after they've been tied. Two strings on one line or two strings on both lines in the middle, there are four strings. Add tape to the cord's endpoints to conceal the broken ends. This would make it easier to add the beads. Congratulations on your achievement. This has been the most complicated part. The rest is only tying easy knots and keeping track of the ends.

- Introduce beads to the Macramé

- Connect one bead to each of the two side cords' rows. Make the bead also by tying a cord on both sides underneath it. Tie a single or (Overhand Knot) about 1/14 inch below the beads with the center of the four strings.

- White mirror with Macramé, beaded mirror with Macramé, plain knotted mirror with Macramé.

- Take one cord from the middle and attach it to the two cords on the ends. Build a knot with the three by wrapping them around each other on both sides. Attach the mirror to get even knot sizes. Add one of the mirror's three side cording to the backend to hold it steady.

- Tie simple ties on all three side cords on the lower left and right of a mirror. Divide the three side cords once more. Place one on either side of the mirror's back to secure it in place, and tie two around the front of the mirror in a knot.

- Enter knots on the back of the Macramé mirror, a quick Macramé mirror tactic.

- Turn the mirror over and tie all of the strings together.

- Delete the front tie by switching the mirror back over it. Slip the back cords into the tie and tighten the knot. Cut the chord's edge to a length of about 14 inches. Fraying occurs as you pull the edges or remove the cording. To fluff the Thread, brush the edges with the brush's edges. Hang it up and take pleasure in it.

Hanging Basket

This basket-style hanger is a multi-functional piece that is equally at home when used as a plant hanger in the conservatory, as a craft caddy in your sewing room, or as a hanging fruit bowl in the kitchen. Alternating square knots create a beautiful net-like pattern for the basket enclosure.

Materials:

- 167m (553ft) length of 2.5mm (1/8in) rope

- 6cm (23/8in) metal ring

- Two 20cm (77/8in) cane rings

- Knots & techniques

- Wrapped Knot

- Square Knot Triple

- Half Hitch Alternating

- Square Knot Pattern

- Overhand Knot Wrapping a Ring

- Mounting Techniques

Preparation:

- Cut forty 4m (131/4ft) lengths of 2.5mm (1/8in) rope

- Cut three 2m (61/2ft) lengths of 2.5mm (1/8in) rope

- Cut one 1m (31/4ft) length of 2.5mm (1/8in) rope

Directions:

- Tie a 2m (612ft) length of rope around the 6cm (238) metal frame.

- Fold the forty 4m (1318) ft lengths of rope in half around the interior of the ring to attach them to the ring.

- Secure all cords together directly under the ring with a 3.5cm (138in) wrapped knot using one of the 2m (612ft) lengths of rope.

- Divide the cords into eight groups of ten cords immediately under the wrapped knot. Each team will now form a sinnet. With each sinnet, repeat steps 5–8.

- On either hand, tie four 10-cord square knots with four filler cords and three working cords.

- Drop down 17cm (634in) and tie one 6-cord square knot with four filler cords and one working cord on either side using the middle six cords.

- Alternate cords and tie two 5-cord square knots, one on either line, using three filler cords and one working cord.

- Directly under, tie another 6-cord square knot for the middle six strings, using four filler cords and one working cord on each hand.

- Lower yourself to 17cm (634in) and tuck all of your cords into the first of your cane loops. The holdings cord will now be made out of the horizontal cane band. Attach each rope to the cane ring with triple-half hitches.

- Tie a series of twenty square knots immediately under the first cane ring to protect it.

- Drop 1.5cm (58in) down, alternating strings, and tie the second row of twenty square knots.

- Work another eight rows in an alternating square knot pattern.

- Tuck all of the cords into the second cane loop. The horizontally placed cane ring will now act as the retaining cord. On the cane ring, tie triple half hitches with each rope.

- Closely gather the rope and draw it upwards until it is level with the cane ring. This will serve as the hanging basket's core. Using the 1m (314ft) length of rope, tie a double overhand knot.

- Tie a 3.5cm (138in) wrapped knot over the top of the double overhand knot with the remaining 2m (612ft) of rope.

- Cut the cords to the size you want.

Macramé Top

Materials:

- Plain white cotton T-shirt (long is better than short)

- Dylon Pink Flamingo Dye

- Salt

- Bucket

- Spoons/stick for stirring

- Small container for mixing dye

- Rubber gloves

- Hanger

Steps:

Step one

Mix the dye as per the manufacturer's Steps: and thoroughly wet the T-shirt. We used half a packet of dye, as we were only dyeing a couple of T-shirts. Choose a 100% cotton garment or one with as high a cotton percentage mix as possible, as human-made fibers such as polyester or viscose won't absorb the dye.

Step two

- Put your T-shirt on a hanger (it's the easiest way to control the dyeing process) and dip it into the dye bath, approximately two-thirds of the way up the shirt, for 30 seconds. This first dip needs to be really quick.

Step three

- For the second dip, put the T-shirt back into the dye bath two-thirds up the dyed section. This time leave for a minute or two. Keep an eye on the color – once you're happy with the Ombre effect that's starting to appear, take the T-shirt out of the bath and rinse the dyed section with warm water. Be careful not to get any pink dye on the white section.

Step four

- Add another tablespoon of dye to the bath and mix thoroughly. Put only the lower third of your T-shirt back in for three or four minutes. Check the Ombre effect – if you think the base needs to be darker, leave it in the bath for a few more minutes. Once happy, rinse the dyed part until the water runs clear and leave to dry.

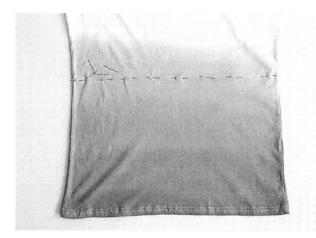

Step five

- Give the T-shirt a good press as you need it to be flat for the next steps. Run a line of pins where you want the top of the macramé section to start – ours began 26cm (10¼") up from the hem.

Step six

- Remove the seams up to where you've pinned by cutting very close to the edge of the stitching. This gives a neat finish.

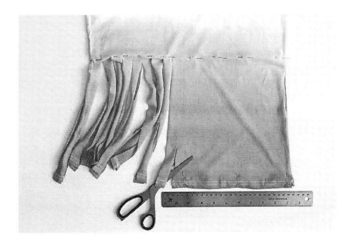

Step seven

- Measure the T-shirt's width and divide by two – this will give you the number of strips you need to cut. If the number is odd, then round down to the nearest even number (you need an equal number of strips, and it's better if they're thicker rather than thinner). Cut the strips up to the pinned line.

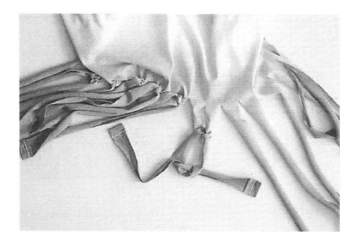

Step eight

- Take the first two strips on the outside edge (we worked left to the right) and tie them together in a double knot. You want the tension to be firm but not over-pulled. Continue knotting in pairs along the whole of the T-shirt front and back.

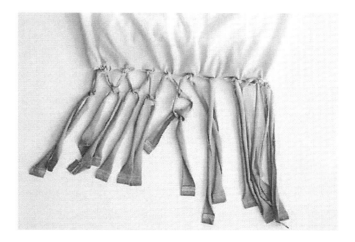

Step nine

- For the next row, take two strips from the next-door knots and knot together 2.5cm (1") below the first row. Continue front and back. You should start to see a triangular shape forming.

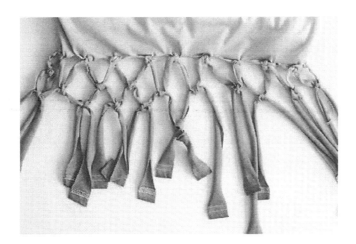

Step ten

- Repeat the above step to create another row of knots. This time a diamond shape will have formed. If you're working with a really long T-shirt, you could add a few more rows of knots – we liked the cropped effect we created, so we kept to just three.

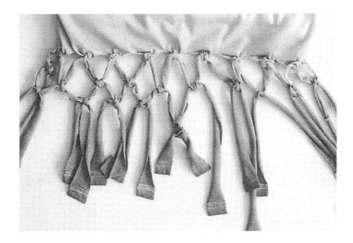

Step eleven

- To finish, cut off the over-locked hem from the bottom of each strip, so they curl up neatly. Now all you need is a sunny day to show it off.

Barefoot Macramé Sandals

Materials:

Pure cotton yarn or macramé cord

Scissors

Large hole beads, for instance: the silver spacer beads.

The Bulldog clips.

Directions:

- Make 3 pieces of yarn or cords about 3m long, then locate the middle point of the strips and make a knot. The yarn must be long; it will be needed for the ankle straps.

- On one of the sides of the knot, braid strands of 2-3 inches together.

- Loose the knot which was earlier made, and tie it again once you've made a spiral loop along with the braided strand. This creates what is called a toe loop of your sandal!

- The major sandal part, which goes down from the ankle to cross the foot's front and then towards the toe, generally, is made using square knots. There are half a dozen strands to use now, so divide them into 3 strands, with each having two strands.

- From the right side, put that strand on top of the one in the middle, making a D-shaped-looking loop. The strand located on the left should be threaded underneath the one in the middle and inside the loop with D-shape.

- To make or create the leading section of the square knot, pull the right and the left strands. In the opposite direction, do the same thing for the left side. Move the strand on the left side over the one in the center, then thread the strand on the right-hand side under the one in the center and backward into the D-shaped loop. Draw the strands on the right and on the left from the one in the middle to finish the first square knot.

- Make two other square knots, in addition to the first square knots tied. Next, thread the round beads made of silver on the strand in the center. Then around this same bead, begin the initial part of the next SK.

- Repeat steps 6 and 7; there should be a total of 10 beads, which would be joined to the center strand with macramé SK. A few more beads are needed for bigger sizes).

- Complete the section with beads by making 1 or 2 plain SK that have no heads and separate the strands in two, with each split having about 3 heads. Braid the strands to form the straps for the ankle till a length/diameter of about 50 centimeters is reached. This will allow you to wrap them around your ankles a few times. Alternatively, another bead made of silver can be added towards the end between an SK for some decoration. When doing this, it is important to make two knots (double knots) towards the bottom part of the final square knot to make it firm. Cut off any remaining unused thread and repeat the steps above to make the sandal's second leg.

DIY Macrame Wall Hanging Mandala Wreath

Materials:

- 10 Inch Ring of Metal

- Cord for macrame-65 yards

- Optional: Wooden beads

- Standard scissors

- Sharp garment scissors for fringe trimming

- Needle for tapestry

- Wire brush for pets or fine comb

Directions:

- Cut 80 cord threads that are 24 inches in length. Every unit requires 8 strands, and for this product, you can make 10 totals.

- Through a lark's head knot, fasten the strands to the metal frame.

- Make a square knot with 4 strands in the middle. For the 4 threads to the right and the 4 threads to the left, now make a square knot.

- Take 2 threads from the far-left square knot to the right and 2 strands from the central square knot to the left and make a square knot. In the 4 threads to the right of the whole new square knot, incorporate a square knot.

- Take the 4 strands in the middle and make the last square knot.

- The time is now for a double half hitch knot. A lead cord will now be the far-right strand. To make the first stitch, take the neighbor's cord and wrap it up and across the lead cord. Make one more to secure into place with the same adjacent strand. Repeat down to the right middle strand.

- Do the same thing on the left-hand side.

- To create the "v" form, continue with the main cord from the right side to the half hitch knot.

- Continue along the right and left sides of this process.

- If you want to close the shape as in the previous round, go ahead and do it now, or we can insert the 2 remaining lead cords with a tapestry needle through a wood bead. With a quick knot, tie it into space.

- Make a rough cut about 1 inch long using the scissors you have on hand.

- Fray off the strands and use a wire pet brush or comb to brush them off.

- To remove the fringe, use your nice scissors so it has a lovely clean cut.

- Complete these 9 more times, and you're done.

Advanced Projects

Chic DIY Plant Hanger

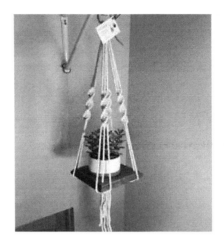

Materials:

- 3 nice, strong, and colorful cords

- Scissors

- 6 wooden beads

- A ring

- A plant vase

Directions:

- Pass 2 cords out of the 3 through the ring, leaving it to go without any pattern for a reasonable distance. Insert 3 beads and knot with a double half-hitch knotting method.

- Insert the beads on the other side and make the same double half-hitch knot.

- Take one cord from each one of the 2 sides and entwine them using the same knotting pattern.

- Do this on the other side too.

- Now leave about 3-inch and knot the cords again.

- Put the plant vase in place. Take the remaining cord and tie the 4 cords neatly and carefully.

- Leave the strands to go down the length of your choice and cut off the extra strands.

- Your chic Macramé DIY plant hanger is ready to be hanged!

Macramé Wedding Arch

Ceremony arches are an ideal way to show your unique look. This DIY Macramé wedding arch is the right design for an outdoor event, incorporating a friendly touch of bohemia. Macramé provides an atmospheric feel with its knotted technique and allows a perfect background for photographs from ceremonies. A Macramé ceremony arch will bring a unique charm to your wedding while keeping it

Directions:

- Follow directions on the box to attach all of your backdrop frame's key parts.

- Spray paint at the backdrop Stand's related parts. When clear, finish setting up the frame for the background.

- Cut the normal cording, so the height of the foreground picture is double that. Fold the cord in 2, and then put the 2 folded over the top handle. Bring the cording ends via the top loop, and pull to lock.

- Continue stage 3 before 10 bits of cording have been added, creating 20 bits.

- Every group of hanging cords has 2 pieces hanging at the bottom. Divide the initial classes into 2, and build new 2 groups. Add these latest classes some 2-inch deep-in knots.

- Continue to move 5 until about 4 vertical rows of knots are joined together.

- Fall the 2 center cording parts off your ties for the next round. From hanging these, 2 items. Once you launch the next round of knots, lower the next row of cording off the knots. Follow this process until you get both sides to the edges of the context.

- Grab scissors, and then remove the loose cording ends. Starting from the middle cut diagonally, so the cord inside is the shortest and the longest outer cording.

- Fill a tub with some water and food coloring, and then put the Macramé's ends in. Squeeze the Macramé and allow it to dry to remove some excess ink.

- After your Macramé has cooled, decorate with fake eucalyptus, the top and side of your ceremony background. Start by wrapping the eucalyptus around the top left of your backdrop, and run them around the pole while you operate. It will hang on to its own, but if not, it should be protected with some floral rope.

- Enhance the backdrop by adding fake peonies to the top corners of the arch for ceremonies. Feed the peony via the eucalyptus, and then use floral wire to tie it to the background.

Macramé Garden Chairs

Are you interested in making a personalized Macramé lawn chair? Decide on the paint and give a special touch to your own lawn chair by retrofitting an old chair with this DIY Macramé lawn chair. Don't throw away those rusty folding lawn chairs; reweave the cover with a brightly colored art string and carry them back to life.

Materials:

- 200 yds. with a 6 mm. Macramé string

- Crochet Hooks 19.00 mm.

- Metal lawn chair frame

- Scissors

- Lighter

- Design

Directions:

- Extract webbing or lining from the chair using scissors. Clean out the case.

- You will want to put your cord roll on the floor within the chair frame to start your rig. It is the cord that is the simplest positioning over the entire weaving cycle. Create a double square knot beginning on the seat bottom ring, leaving around 6-inch of slack at the top. Bear in mind that you can just thread on the straight sectors of the frame of your chair, leaving the rounded edges empty.

- Now pick up your chair below the center bar and up over the frame end. Then, thread the rope around the chair frame and draw it outwards. Move the crochet hook into the loop you have just created. Push the rope firmly, ensuring that the thread does not come free. Often, to ensure you can bring the hook in the next time around, make sure that the loop lies on the fattest portion of the line. Trust me, when you proceed, this will make your life a lot simpler.

- Put the chord back at the bottom, underneath the center plate, and then over the seat frame top. Wrap the rope around the frame and slide it under the first pair of cords to the edge. Push the crochet hook into the loop much as you did before, letting it lie on the flat portion of the thread. Tightly grab the loose thread, and proceed.

Macramé Multi-Plant Hanger

You can create a plant hanger with Macramé in several styles. Many instructions are much more difficult and time-consuming to execute, however. These Macramé plant hanger patterns for newcomers are a great starting point if you want to create anything convenient and straightforward.

Such DIY Macramé plant hangers come in many sizes and types, and with little or no practice, each design is easy enough to complete. Several creative embellishments render your Macramé project appear customer and more polished. It is nice to practice some simple Macramé knots on some unused rope parts first before you make a plant hanger. Understanding the ties can make Macramé's directions far simpler to grasp.

Directions:

- Bring all 8 pieces of cord together, split in half, and loop around the pipe.

- Utilizing your 5 ft. long string piece, tie a knot in a loop right under the band.

- Take 4 strands and tie one knot in a square. Repeat 6 times.

- Repeat this pattern for the next 4-cord group; repeat with the residual cords.

- Leave a distance of 2 ½ cm. and make a knot of half-square.

- Repeat until a 5-inch spiral has been formed.

- Follow the sequence with the remaining groups of knots.

- Leave a 6-inch distance to build a square crossover knot utilizing the first group's 2 right cords, and the neighboring group's 2 left cords.

- Repeat with classes left in the knot.

- Leave a 6-inch gap and build another square knot crossover by reversing the cords from the prior stage.

- Leave a distance of 3 ½-inch and make a knot at the circle.

- Trim extra cord to produce a finish on the tassel.

Ways to Decorate your Plant Hanger

Now that you have developed your simple plant hanger for Macramé, here are 2 innovative ways you can carve them up and render them your own:

Dip-Dyed Plant Hanger

Dip dying is a simple way to give your Macramé plant hanger a splash of color. Note, the further you dip it in the reaction mixture, the deeper the hue.

You can soak-dye your Macramé plant hanger in 5 simple measures here:

Arrange dye solution as indicated by the box. Assure that you are utilizing a glass container or a cup to avoid staining.
Gently tap the hanger until 1/3 of the circumference is immersed into the water.

Thread over a wooden dowel, the upper part of the plant hanger, and position over the container or bowl gap. It should leave the hanger hanging while the bottom portion is painted. Hang on for 30 minutes.
Take the hanger from the solvent for the dyeing. Rinse out the residual pigment in the warm spray. Rinse the bottom, before pure water runs.

Let dry absolutely.

Embroidered Plant Hanger

Another imaginative way to dress things up is to tie the embroidery floss across your Macramé plant hanger. Build your own unique designs with different patterns and colors.

Lay at the bottom a bit of embroidery and then fold around it. Continue until protected by target duration.

Use a wooden stick or toothpick to split the floss and tuck in the loose part into the wrapped component to finish the part.
To conclude the sequence, replicate this with certain colors.

Macramé Shopping Bag

Directions:

- Cut 10 ropes 2.3 meters in length. Fold half and fill the middle of the folded handle with the void. Take the ends of the rope and cross the last step of the loop you made. Pull close and strong. Continue to attach five pieces of cord to each bag handle.

- Separate two rope bits at one end and move the remaining rope to the other. We will make the first knot with these two parts. Turn the left corner in the right corner and make a curve. Take a left (still straight) rope and fill the room with the two ropes you made. Remove the two corners until the knot is rising and in the right place. You want the handle to be around 5 cm in length. Take the left-hand rope, and this time put it right to complete the knot. This time, thread through the gap the right-side rope. Bring the knot tight again.

- Create four more knots in a row on the handle with the rest of the ropes. Continue again, but the first rope is missing this time and the second and third one's tie. Continue along the route. Make four knots this time, and do not knot the first or the last rope.

- When the second row is done, make the third row the same as the first (five knots without missing ropes).

- Upon completing the third section, repeat Steps 2-4 in the second handle.

After that, bring the two handles face to face together.

- Take both end ropes from the front of the bag and back to begin the next row.

- Fasten the ties on the front and back on the other end. You are then faced with the last lines on the front and back. Tie these together.

- Knot until the strands are around 10 cm left of the rope.

- Cut 4 meters in length of the rope. Use the same technique to tie it to the last knot of the handle.

- Take the front and back strand and wrap the cord around. Place a double hitch knot and take two additional knots, one on the front and the other on the back.

- Taking off the hanging rope. Link these strands instead of knots. You should apply some glue to cover them. Put it together to make a sheet.

Clutch Purse

A handmade macramé clutch purse is a sure-fire way to impress your friends on a night out on the town, and it's just the right size to carry your party essentials. With its pretty chevron flap and magnetic button closure, it is a must-have fashion accessory.

Materials:

- 54m (180ft) length of 3mm (1⁄8in) jute

- 56m (186½ft) length of 3mm (1⁄8in) rope

- Hot glue gun

- Three 18mm (11⁄16in) magnetic snap fasteners

Knots & Techniques:

- Reverse Lark's Head Knot

- Square Knot

- Alternating Square Knot Pattern

- Decreasing Square Knot Pattern

- Diagonal Double Half Hitch

- Overhand Knot

- Numbering Cords

- Weaving Finish

- Lacing Up

Preparation:

- Cut eighteen 3m (10ft) lengths of 3mm (1⁄8in) jute

- Cut eighteen 3m (10ft) lengths of 3mm (1⁄8in) rope

- Cut one 2m (61⁄2ft) length of 3mm (1⁄8in) rope

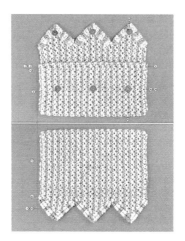

Directions:

- Secure the 2m (6½ft) length of rope to a project board with T-pins, making sure it is straight and firm. This becomes your holding cord.

- Alternating lengths of jute with lengths of rope, mount the eighteen 3m (10ft) lengths of jute and the eighteen 3m (10ft) lengths of rope onto the holding cord using reverse lark's head knots. The width of the mounted cords should be 24.5cm (9¾in), and they should be centered on the holding cord.

- Directly beneath the holding cord, tie a row of eighteen square knots.

- Alternate cords and tie a row of seventeen square knots.

- Continue an alternating square knot pattern with no spaces in between the rows for another forty-five rows, ending with a row of eighteen square knots. The total length of the macramé should be 27cm (10⅝in); if necessary, work more rows of square knots to bring the macramé to the required length, but remember it is important to end with a row of eighteen square knots.

- Divide the cords into three groups of twenty-four cords: group 1 – cords 1–24; group 2 – cords 25–48; and group 3 – cords 49–72. Complete steps 7– 15 on each of the three groups of cords to create what will be the front flap chevron edge on the finished bag.

- On each of the three groups of cords, work a decreasing square knot pattern directly beneath the last row tied, beginning with six square knots and finishing with one square knot in the last row.

- Number the cords in each of the three groups 1 to 24.

- Make cord 1 a holding cord; bring it down diagonally left to right along the edge of the pattern to sit directly beneath the single square knot and tie diagonal double half hitches with cords 2–12.

- Make cord 24 a holding cord; bring it down diagonally right to left along the edge of the pattern to sit directly beneath the single square knot and tie diagonal double half hitches with cords 13–23.

- Cross over the holding cords (cords 1 and 24) so that they swap positions.

- Now renumber the cords in each group 1 to 24.
- Make cord 1 a holding cord; bring it down left to the right, so it sits directly beneath the row of diagonal double half hitches, and tie diagonal double half hitches with cords 2–12.

- Make cord 24 a holding cord; bring it down right to left, so it sits directly beneath the row of diagonal double half hitches, and tie diagonal double half hitches with cords 13–23.

- Tie holding cords 1 and 24 together with a double overhand knot.

- Remove the macramé from the project board. Flip the macramé over and use the weaving finish technique to conceal the cords along the chevron edge. (Do not trim the holding cord along the straight edge.)

- Trim the cords in each group to 5mm (1⁄4in) and use a hot glue gun to secure them down.

- To make your macramé into a clutch bag, keep the macramé's wrong side facing up but orientate it so that the chevrons are at the top and the straight edge is at the bottom. Fold the bottom edge up by 12cm (43⁄4in) to make the pocket of the bag.

- Use the holding cord for lacing up the sides of the bag pocket, finishing with the cord on the inside of the purse, and securing with a double overhand knot.

- Attach the magnetic snap fasteners to complete the purse. Use a hot glue gun to secure one part of each to the backside of the chevrons and the matching part to the front of the bag pocket, so that they match up when the flap is closed.

Baby Pendant Lantern

The open latticework of Moroccan lanterns has inspired the shape of this beautiful decoration, and it will provide you with a beautiful feature anywhere in your home. It could be styled as a mobile in a baby's nursery or to hung as a decorative piece alongside your hanging planters.

Materials:

- 106m (351ft) length of 5mm (1/4in) rope

- 2.5cm (1in) metal ring

- Cane rings: one 10cm (4in); one 13cm (5in); two 20cm (8in)

Knots & Techniques:

- Double Half Hitch

- Reverse Lark's Head Knot

- Square Knot

- Triple Half Hitch

Preparation:

- Cut twenty-four 4m (131/4ft) lengths of 5mm (1/4in) rope

- Cut two 5m (161/2ft) lengths of 5mm (1/4in) rope

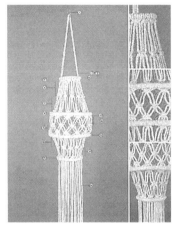

Directions:

- Take both of the 5m (16½ft) lengths of rope and fold them in half over the inside of the metal ring to give you four equal lengths of rope hanging down.

- Place all four cords inside the 10cm (4in) cane ring. The cane ring sitting horizontally is now to be used as the holding cord.

- Take two adjacent cords, drop down 30cm (12in) and tie the cords onto the ring with double half hitches. Repeat to tie the remaining two cords onto the opposite side of the cane ring.

- Attach twenty-four of the 4m (13 1/4ft) lengths of rope to the cane ring – twelve cords to each half – using reverse lark's head knot.

- Secure the cords to the ring by tying a row of thirteen square knots directly beneath the cane ring.

- Alternate cords, drop down 7cm (2 3/4in), and tie a row of thirteen square knots.

- Alternate cords, drop down 7cm (2 3/4in), and tie another row of thirteen square knots.

- Place all cords inside one of the 20cm (8in) cane rings. This cane ring sitting horizontally is now to be used as the holding cord. Tie all cords onto the cane ring using triple-half hitches.

- Secure the cords to the cane ring by tying a row of thirteen square knots directly beneath.

- Alternate cords, drop down 3cm (1 1/8in), and tie a row of thirteen square knots.

- Alternate cords, drop down 3cm (1 1/8in) and tie another row of thirteen square knots.

- Repeat steps 8 and 9 with the second 20cm (8in) cane ring.

- Alternate cords, drop down 4.5cm (1 3/4in), and tie a row of thirteen square knots.

- Alternate cords, drop down 4.5cm (1 3/4in), and tie another row of thirteen square knots.

- Place all cords inside the 13cm (5in) cane ring. This cane ring sitting horizontally is now to be used as the holding cord. Tie all cords onto the cane ring using double half hitches.

- Trim the cords to 65cm (25 1/2in) or to your desired length.

CHAPTER 11

HOW TO SUCCEED IN CREATING YOUR PROJECT

Do Not Go Overboard in the Crafting Aisle

It is beautiful, right? All the fluffy balls of yarn and shiny needles glittering in front of you? Do you envision yourself sitting comfortably, knitting with your beautiful needles, and creating gorgeous gifts?

As you wander down the aisle, lightly passing your fingertips over the differently textured wools, you picture all the beautiful crafts you will be making for your friends and family. Several hundred dollars later and crafting room or box overflowing with new toys, it hits you that you have no clue what to start with or what you want to do. Or you start on a project and hate the way aluminum needles feel in your hand, but every time you touch the bamboo needles your friend uses, you swoon. You have a pile of notions you never touch but are always running back to the store to grab just one more of that one thing you use all the time. Save yourself the heartache and hassle, pick up a few of the basics to start, and then add on as you try new techniques or tools.

Save Your Money... in the Beginning

The pretty, sparkly, and colorful yarn is attractive. When it is soft or has a great texture, you just want to run your hands over it again and again. As you begin learning, you will be knitting and removing stitches, creating a lot of wear and tear on the yarn. All the pretty glitter and texture will be shredded.

Your yarn will tangle—not a fun way to start your knitting experience. You are going to stretch out your first few yarns, so plan on investing in a good synthetic yarn that is inexpensive. Save those pretty yarns for when you are more experienced. Part of the joy of your later projects will be running to the store to pick up a flashy, fun, funky ball of yarn and revel in the joy of working with it, preserving the character of the fibers. Test your skills on cheap yarns so you can flex your creative muscles with the pricey ones.

Side note: just do not buy the super cheap acrylic yarn. This does not work well for many projects, especially novice ones. Instead, opt for a simple natural fiber.

Befriend the Basics

Again, keep your distance from the bedazzled choices of yarn. These are not good starter yarns. Instead, buddy up to the basic options.

Flex your creative muscle with a bold color choice if you have a hard time accepting the simplicity at this point but try to keep the color light. The important thing is that you see your stitches as you practice, and a lighter yarn color will make it more apparent when you miss a stitch or make a mistake.

Get Curious About New Ideas

The beauty of knitting today is that there is a plethora of techniques and options out there for you to experiment with. As you are learning, now is a great time to try out some fun ideas. When you are following a pattern, and it throws a challenge at you, give it a shot. Directions for cables and yarns over may scare you at first, but when you get into them, you will find they are not that bad. Plus, did you start knitting for just simple scarves? Probably not! So, this is the time to conquer your fear of a decrease and knit those beautiful hats.

Search for Inspiration and Enjoy the Creativity

Scour Pinterest, stalk knitting blogs, browse images of knitted projects to become inspired with what you will knit one day. Think about expanding your repertoire of knitting projects to include headbands, gloves, and other fun "newbie" projects. Many sites will allow you to search their pattern database by skill level so you can find projects that you can complete at this stage and droll over projects that you want to challenge yourself with as you keep practicing. This not only helps you find new projects but when frustration and boredom kick in, you can scroll through your favorite places to reignite the dream you have of becoming a glorious knitter.

Use Your Resources

If you are getting frustrated with something, check out the pages of this book for tips on how to accomplish it, or spend a few minutes on YouTube watching a video to nail that purl. You do not need to suffer alone. This and other resources are out there to get you to where you want to be. All else fails. Throw it in a bag and take it into your local yarn shop and get some advice! Maybe join a knitting group in the area, so you have a community of knitters to help you learn the tricks of the trade.

Put It Away Before Someone (Or Something) Gets Hurt!

You have knitted and removed stitches for what feels like hours and are still not past the first row of stitches. You just want to throw it and cry. Take a deep breath—this has happened (and often still does) to all of us. Put your knitting aside, take a little (or a lot) time to yourself, and then go back at it again when you are ready. If you try to power through the frustration, you will probably contract "crazy knitter fit" and will infect your project with it. You will get so annoyed with the one slipped stitch that you will keep making the same mistake throughout the project, and it rarely ends well. Coming at the problem with calm and rested eyes will often help you solve the problem, at least easier than before, and get you moving again.

Know Your Abbreviations or at Least Have a Cheat Sheet Handy

As you progress in your knitting career, you will probably move on to patterns. Many of your designs will explain the abbreviations they use, but some will not. If you do not have much experience with knitting patterns, it may look like gibberish to you. This is a simple fix: keep a list of abbreviations and a short description of what they are. Add new terms and stitches to the list as you go. Stash this list in your knitting supplies so you can add or reference it as you are working.

Hold on to Your Practice Projects

As you are learning, you will have plenty of projects that just do not turn out showcase-worthy. That is normal and a good thing.
But instead of tossing those practice projects, consider taking them apart to reuse the yarn for another project or using parts of them in a new craft if there are salvageable pieces. Upcycle or recycle these projects later as you become more skilled. Even when you are a knitter, either intermediate or advanced, you will have practice projects and money in the long run.

Knitting can be relaxing and fun, or you could let it stress you out and cause anxiety. You should choose knitting for the latter. So, what if you mess up? Laugh it off! Knitting takes time and practice, so the more you learn from it, the better you will get. Enjoy the ride. You can lose yourself in repetition, and you can challenge yourself with new ideas. Venture out and try it; you will be surprised at how quickly you will turn from thinking this is too difficult to, "Is this all it is?!"

CHAPTER 12

GLOSSARY

There are many ways that people refer to knots and cords as they go through making a project. I have tried to put together a list of commonly used terms you will encounter as you read patterns or watch tutorial videos.

- **Alternating** — Using two cords from an earlier knot with two cords from another prior knot to form a new knot.

- **Alternating square knots** — When you alternate the sides of your square knots. A left-half square knot, then a right half square knot.

- **ASK** — Alternating knots of the square. Starting from the left, and then starting from the right, or vice versa.

- **Bar**—An elevated segment created by a certain knot. Half hitch knots are sometimes used to create bars. These can run horizontally, vertically, or diagonally.

- **Body** — The main part of the project.

- **Braid/Plait** — ree or four cords or groups of cords.

- **Braided cord** — A type of cord made from several thinner pieces of cord woven together.

- **Knot button** — A tight, round decorative knot.

- **BH** —T he button's door/hole. Creating a loop that could be used for fastening or joining parts.

- **Crown knot** — A decorative knot, sometimes called the "Chinese flower" or "Shamrock knot" because it looks like a flower when finished.

- **Combination knot/knots of fusion** — A new or nonstandard type of knot, using a combination of two or more knots.

- **Cords** — Cords are any fiber material that is used to make projects.

- **Core/Fillers/Knot-bearing** — The cord(s) running through a project's center and knotting around it. These are sometimes referred to as 'fillers' or cords.

- **Crook** — The curved parts of a cord loop.

- **Diameter** — The width of a cord, usually given in millimeters.

- **DHH** — Half hitch double. Connecting two knots of half-hitch.

- **Finishing knot** — A knot tied to secure the ends of the cord and to prevent them from unraveling.

- **Fringe** — Cord ends lengths not knotted, but left as is or combed out.

- **Gusset** — A term used to join a project's sides together, like a bag.

- **Interlace** — A pattern in which cords are intertwined and woven together instead of knotted.

- **Knotting cord/Working cord** — The cord you manipulate to tie the knots.

- **LH** — Lark's Head knot.

- **Loop** — The circular or oval shape created by folding the cord in half.

- **Micro-Macramé** — Macramé projects made using materials that are delicate or small in diameter. Usually 2 mm or less, such as floss or hemp.

- **Mount** — An object that is used as part of a Macramé project, such as a brace, frame, or handles.

- **Natural** — When used to describe cords, it refers to any material made from plants, wood, and other natural substances, such as hemp and cotton.

- **Netting** — A series of knots with open spaces between them. Often used to create bags and plant hangers

- **OH** — Overhand knot.

- **Scallops** — Knot loops created along the edges of a project.

- **Segment** — A unit of a project that uses common knots, cord, or design.

- **Sennit/Sinnet** — A single chain of identical knots.

- **Standing end** — The cord end that is secured on a Macramé board or other surface and is not used to build knots.

- **SK** — Square knot.

- **Synthetic** — When used to describe cords, it refers to man-made fibers, such as polypropylene and nylon.

- **Weaving** — Weaving cords means placing them under each other or over each other.

- **Working cord/Knotting cord** — The cord with which you are currently working.

CONCLUSION

At the end of this book, I'd like to share with you the most common mistakes I've encountered in my experience as a Macramé project maker and how to fix them. They are as follows:

Error 1: When Tying a Knot, Doing It in a Sloppy Way

How to Fix:

- Hold the cord under the 6-inch mark (junction) with your left hand and the cord end facing upward on top of your right hand.

- Bend both hands inward, making sure the cords are at the same level and are under pressure before tying the knot.

- Pull-on both ends of the cord to tighten the knot before cutting off the excess part of both cords.

Error 2: Not Making the Cord Longer When Making a Knot

How to Fix:

- Keep tension on the knot, 1-2 inches higher than the knot itself.

- Pull both ends of the cord to pull it in; this will reduce any stress caused by the knot, resulting in more durability for your cord and fastening knots well.

Error 3: Not Using Enough Tension While Tying Knots and Cords Together

How to Fix:

- When tying a new cord to an existing rope, tighten it under pressure, don't let it flop around loosely.

- When adding another loop of cord to an existing rope, make sure that you pull fairly hard on all ends of both cords before joining them together.

- When adding one or more cords to an existing cord, regulate the pressure so that both cords are under equal tension at all times.

Error 4: Not Using the Right Type of Knot for a Certain Macramé Project

How to Fix:

- Using a Granny knot for decorative purposes only and not for fastening rope together.

- Use a Lark's Head knot for an 8-in-1 or 6-in-1 when you should have used an Overhand knot.

- Use an Overhand knot when you should have used an Overhand Loop Knot.

- And many others too...

How can you prevent making Macramé mistakes?

Read and understand the instructions carefully before starting a project.

IMPORTANT: Do all the knots slowly and carefully, don't be in a hurry or just "wing it."

Be enduring with yourself; this is not some kind of race, so take your time to do things properly and neatly.

Similarly, it helps if you have somebody who is experienced in Macramé nearby to assist whenever you get stuck in doing a certain knot or technique.

Lastly, is to keep a positive attitude in doing projects. Any time you find yourself getting frustrated with how a project is going, stop, walk away and take a break from it. You can at all times come back to it later and start again when you are calm again. Remember, this is not something you finish overnight, nor should you pressure yourself to finish it as fast as possible since the result will be more satisfying when done correctly and neatly.

Thank you for reading this book, and I hope you enjoy doing Macramé!

Good Luck with your Macramé Projects!

Made in the USA
Las Vegas, NV
04 May 2022

48405898R00085